JN417476

C.T. STUDD

Man of Faith

C.T. STUDD

C.T. STUDD
Man of Faith

By
NORMAN P. GRUBB

WEC Publications
Seoul Korea 2018

◆ ◆ ◆

He climbed the steep ascent of heaven
Through peril, toil, and pain ; O
God, to us may grace be given To
follow in his train.

◆ ◆ ◆

FOREWORD

What a man! This book tells the story of a man who was fabulously rich, but died in Africa with virtually nothing, who had celebrity status in his day as a sportsman, but gave it all up for Jesus–all in order that others who had never heard the Good News of Jesus in China, India and Africa might be enriched.

For many years I have served in the Mission God led him to found. He gave us in WEC a vision to go to the least evangelized parts of the world, a faith to tackle the impossible, a passion for holy living and a commitment to work with like-minded co–labourers to complete the task Jesus gave us. His legacy is huge and extends to today. Norman Grubb, CT's successor, and author of this book continued the moulding of WEC's spiritual life and mission vision. His writings deeply impacted me in my early years while serving with another mission in Africa. In his latter years he also became a friend and mentor to me and my wife, Jill, after I was invited to become a WECer myself. I have now had the honour of serving as a WECer for 40 years!

So I commend this book to you who pick this book up. May it inspire you to great exploits of faith and ministry and hasten the return of our Lord and King!

Patrick Johnstone
WEC International
Author, Operation World

FOREWORD

Sometimes our souls need stirring, our passion needs rekindling, and our faith needs deepening. The amazing story of CT Studd has done this for countless readers, myself included. It is the story of a remarkable man following a remarkable Christ.

In the words of his earliest colleague and son–in–law, Alfred Buxton, CT Studd was a man of "courage in any emergency, determination never to sound the retreat, conviction that he was in God's will, and faith that God would see him through".

But it is also the story of a real person, with strengths and weaknesses like us. Through it, we learn what God can do with a completely surrendered life. We see afresh the trustworthiness of Christ, who was the focus of CT's faith. Christ is worthy of our absolute trust and CT Studd trusted Christ absolutely. Read this book and let God rekindle your passion, deepen your faith in the trustworthiness of Christ, and stir your soul to follow Christ completely.

Louis Sutton
International Director of WEC

FOREWORD

CT Studd, the founder of WEC Mission, has had a tremendous ripple effect on the mission world. His genuine heart to serve the Lord has inspired thousands of missionaries to go out into the unevangelized world and passionately spread the gospel. They have ardently followed the example of CT Studd, whose life reflected true sacrifice and countless joys and tears for the sake of Jesus Christ.

I believe that this book is an invaluable asset to anyone who is burdened by the reality that countless lives are being lost without having the chance to hear the good news of Jesus Christ. I pray that this text will awaken the hearts of missionaries who may have lost sight of the raw sacrifice that the Cross really calls for.

I would also like to recognize the author, Norman Grubb, who so authentically captured Studd's life story and left behind this timeless reference for all those in the mission world. All praise and glory to Jesus Christ our savior and God.

Byung Kook Yoo
Director of International Mission Mobilization of WEC

FOREWORD

BY ALFRED B. BUXTON

C.T. Studd's co–pioneer in the heart of Africa

C. T.'s life stands as some rugged Gibraltar–a sign to all succeeding generations that it is worth while to lose all this world can offer and stake everything on the world to come. His life will be an eternal rebuke to easy–going Christianity. He has demonstrated what it means to follow Christ without counting the cost and without looking back.

C.T. was essentially a cavalry leader, and in that capacity he led several splendid charges. Three in particular stand out : when C.T. and Stanley Smith led forth the Cambridge Seven to China, in 1885; ten years later when C.T. toured the American Universities at the start of the Student Volunteers; and when in 1910 he initiated the campaign for the region between the Nile and Lake Chad (the largest unevangelized region in Africa at the time).

These three things alone have affected missionary history, and through them C. T. for warded evangelization to an extent that we cannot properly gauge. These were his direct work, but the indirect influence which he exerted and which extended in ever widening circles round the world probably accomplished even more. He impersonated the heroic spirit, the apostolic abandon, which it is easy to lose from the work of Christ.

A cavalry leader cannot have all the gifts of an administrator, or he would not have the qualities necessary to lead a charge. In this simple fact is the explanation of the shortcomings some might point out. If there were these, they were in reality the exaggeration of C.T.'s unique qualities : his courage in any emergency, his determination never to sound the retreat, his conviction that he was in God's will, his faith that God would see him through, his contempt of the arm of the flesh, and his willingness to risk all for Christ.

But these are only as Froude wrote of Carlyle, "the mists that hang about a mountain." Men who want no mists must be content with plains. But give me the mountain! It will be but a little while, and, the mists evaporated, the mountain will stand out in all its grandeur.

I myself owe an enormous debt to him. From him I learned that God's ideal of a saint is not a man primarily concerned with his own sanctification : God's saint is 50 percent, a soldier. So we and thousands more will continue to thank God for the soldier life he lived and the soldier death he died. A little time ago I sent him these lines, and how wonderfully they are fulfilled in his case :

Let the victors when they come,
When the forts of folly fall,
Find thy body near the wall.

Now it is for us to try and emulate him. That is the epitaph he would value most.

PREFACE

BY ALFRED B. BUXTON

C.T. Studd's co–pioneer in the heart of Africa

Nothing can really take the place of honest auto biography. But unfortunately "C.T." has left no written record of his life. However, his mother and wife did the next best thing by preserving all his correspondence from boyhood. My object has been to weld these letters into the nearest things to an autobiography. My one qualification for attempting this work is that the convictions which dominated C.T.'s life are also my convictions, and that therefore this book has been written with my heart as well as with my head. He lived to glorify his Saviour. The object of this book is likewise to glorify Him as He is seen at work in and through this utterly surrendered life.

N.P. GRUBB.

17 Highland Road, Norwood,
London, S.E. 19.

CONTENTS

ILLUSTRATIONS

C.T. STUDD

Man of Faith

CHAPTER I

A VISIT TO A THEATRE AND ITS CONSEQUENCES

THE Punchestown Races were over. Crowds were re turning homeward from the famous Irish Derby by train and cross–channel boat. Among them was a wealthy re tired planter. He hurried to Kingstown Harbour, but ar rived five minutes too late to catch the boat. There was nothing else for him to do but to stay the night in Dublin. He was at a loose end, and not knowing how to spend the evening, took a stroll. He noticed over a theatre the names "D.L. Moody and Ira D. Sankey," wondered what Vaudeville Company this was, and went in to have the surprise of his life! He was amazed to find the place crowded out, and on the platform a number of people in ordinary dress and a man singing. He had a wonderful voice, and was singing words such as he had never heard before, As the refrain came again and again with each verse of the hymn :

"There were ninety and nine that safely lay,
In the shelter of the fold,
But one was out on the hills away,
Far off from the gates of gold,"

he stood absolutely riveted. The hymn over, he sat down and heard Moody preach, and strange to relate, instead of going back home next day, he stayed on day after day. Finally, one evening he followed a great throng of people who rose to go into the Enquiry Room. Moody knelt beside him and simply said,

"Mr. Vincent, do you believe Jesus Christ died for you?" "I do," he replied. "Then," said Moody, "thank Him." He did, and he left that room a transformed man.

Mr. Vincent had a great friend, Mr. Edward Studd, also a retired planter. He had made a fortune in India and had come back to England to spend it. He was very fond of sport of all kinds. He went into regular training to go fox–hunting, and was Master of the Hounds. His sons were almost born in the saddle. They went hunting at five and six years of age, strapped to the saddle, and each in his little red coat, and that in Leicestershire, supposed to have the stiffest fences of any country in England. Leaving Hallaton Hall, he bought a large place in Wiltshire, Tedworth, now Tidworth, well known to all soldiers. Here he turned a paddock into a firstrate cricket ground. These were the days when country-house cricket was at its height, and, throughout the summer, matches and cricket weeks were arranged. But, above all, he was an enthusiast on horse–racing. To begin with, he was passionately fond of horses, and when he saw fine horses, he would buy and train, and then race them. He made a racecourse at Tedworth and kept a stud of about twenty horses. He won several steeplechases, but achieved his great ambition when he won the Grand National with a horse called Salamander. It was an unexpected victory and congratulations (and begging letters!) were showered on him, the family celebrating the occasion with a special dinner in Town.

After the Dublin Mission had finished, Moody and Sankey came to London. "Nobody believed very much at that time in a man getting up to preach the Gospel unless he had two things–the tit le of Reverend, and a white tie round his neck. The papers could not understand such a preacher as Mr. Moody, who had neither, and of course they printed column after column against him. But they could not help seeing that he could get more people to his meetings than half a dozen archbishops, and that more were converted than by twenty ordinary ministers. Of course they did not put the right construction on things. They said that Mr. Sankey had come over to sell organs and Mr. Moody to sell his hymn–books." Mr. Studd read the papers day after day, and these things tickled him immensely. One evening he threw the paper down and said, "Well, anyhow, when this man comes to London, I am going to hear him. There must be some good about the man, or he would never be abused so much by the papers."

At this same period Mr. Studd bought a horse that was better than any he had ever owned, and entered him for one of the big races. So certain was he of winning, that he wrote to his friend Mr. Vincent and said, "If you are a wise man, you will come to the race, and put every penny you can on my horse."

A few days later he went up to Town and met his friend. As they drove along in the carriage, Mr. Studd talked of nothing but this horse. They went to Tattersall's. After he had finished his business, he came back to Mr. Vincent and said, "How much money have you put on my horse?" "Nothing." "You are the biggest fool I ever saw," said Mr. Studd. "Didn't I tell you what a good horse he was? But though you are a fool, come along and dine with me; my family are all in the country, and you shall say where we shall go after dinner." Dinner over, Mr. Studd asked, "Now where shall we go to amuse ourselves?" Mr. Vincent suggested Drury Lane Theatre. "What?" said Mr. Studd, "Isn't that where those fellows Moody and Sankey are? Oh, no this isn't Sunday. We will go to the theatre or a concert." "No," said Mr. Vincent, "you are a man of your word, and you said you would go where I chose." With very bad grace he went. On reaching the theatre, it was crowded out and there were no seats left except special ones. But Mr. Vincent was determined to hold on to his prey, so taking out a card case, he wrote hastily on a card to an usher whom he knew. "Come to a certain door and get us in.

I have a wealthy sporting gentleman with me, but I will never get him here again if we do not get a seat." The man came, got them in by the green–room door, across the stage, and plumped them down just under Moody's nose. Mr. Studd never took his eyes off Moody until he had finished his address. Afterwards he said, "I will come and hear this man again. He has just told me everything I have ever done." He kept his word and went again, until he was right soundly converted.

"In the afternoon of that day," wrote one of his sons later, "Father had been full of a thing that takes more possession of a man's heart and head than anything else, the passion for horseracing; and in the evening he was a changed man. Of course he could not go on living the same life as before. He could not go to balls, card parties and all that sort of thing. His conscience told him so. So he decided to go and have it out with Mr. Moody. He went to him and said, 'I want to be straight with you.

Now I am a Christian, shall I have to give up racing and shooting and hunting and theatres and balls?" 'Well,' said Mr. Moody, "Mr. Sutdd, you have been straight with me; I will be straight with you. Racing mean betting, and betting means gambling, and I don't see how a gambler is going to be a Christian. Do the other things as long as you like.' Father asked him again about the theatre and cards, and Moody said, "Mr. Studd, you have children and people you love; you are now a saved man yourself, and you want to get them saved. God will give you some souls, and as soon as ever you have won a soul, you won't care about any of the other things.' Sure enough, to the astonishment of his children and many others, he didn't care for any of these things any longer; but only cared about one thing, and that was saving souls.

"He withdrew from the Turf, giving a racehorse to each of his elder sons as a hunter, and then sold the remainder. He cleared out the large hall of his house at Tedworth, furnished it with chairs and benches, and used to get splendid fellows down from London, merchants and business men, to preach the Gospel to the people. He used to ride round the country and invite and urge the people to come, and come they did in hundreds."

The coachman put what had happened in a nutshell. A guest remarked to him that he had "heard that Mr. Studd had become religious, or something." "Well, sir, said he, "We don't know much about that, but all I can say is that though there's the same skin, there's a new man inside!"

Mr. Studd only lived two years after this. His death came about in a remarkable manner. He was on his way to one of Moody's meetings, and stopped the carriage suddenly, as he had forgotten to bring one of his grooms to the meeting. He alighted and told the rest to drive on. It was late, so he ran all the way back and broke a blood–vessel in his leg. He never recovered from this, but as the clergyman said, who preached the sermon at his funeral, "He did more in two years than most Christians do in twenty." He wrote to his friends when he couldn't speak to them, and sometimes received pretty terse replies. He spoke fearlessly to anyone and everyone. One man, who kept a shop in Regent Street, was a thorough–going agnostic; Mr. Studd was the only man who ever had the courage to speak to him about his soul, and his son said afterwards, "I never remember my father so angry in his life at being so faithfully dealt with!"

CHAPTER II

THREE ETONIANS GET A SHOCK

IS three eldest boys were at Eton, Kynaston, George and Charles. All three brothers got their XI the year of their father's conversion in 1877. So far as is known, this is the only time three brothers were ever in the Eton XI together. They hadn't heard what had happened to their father, and so when, in the middle of the term, he wrote and told them that he had arranged for them to come and meet him in Town, they thought he was going to take them to a theatre or the Christy Minstrels. They got a shock when they found it was a "Pi–show!" He took them to hear Moody. "Before that time," Charlie said later on, "I used to think that religion was a Sunday thing, like one's Sunday clothes, to be put away on Monday morning. We boys were brought up to go to Church regularly, but, although we had a kind of religion, it didn't amount to much. It was just like having a toothache. We were always sorry to have Sunday come, and glad when it was Monday morning.

The Sabbath was the dullest day of the whole week, and just because we had got hold of the wrong end of religion. Then all at once I had the good fortune to meet a real live play–the–game Christian. It was my own father. But it did make one's hair stand on end. Everyone in the house had a dog's life of it until they were converted. I was not altogether pleased with him. He used to come into my room at night and ask if I was converted. After a time I used to sham sleep when I saw the door open, and in the day I crept round the other side of the house when I saw him coming."

A year passed. The boys were home fo r the summer holidays at Tedworth and a number of Cricket matches had been arranged. As usual, their father had men staying in the house each weekend to speak at the meeting on Sunday. Two were down one week–end, one of them was popular with the boys and the other, Mr. W., was not, for they considered him a "milk sop." On the Saturday morning they planned a trick on him. They asked him to go for a ride with them and their father, for they had discovered that, although he said he could ride, he was really no good at it. The three boys rode behind, and suddenly passed the other two, cantering like the wind, and of course nothing could hold the horses–to the great discomfort of Mr. W. He, however, had more mettle than he appeared to have, and kept his seat. They repeated this several times and their father could not rebuke them, because he was bursting with laughter himself.

But that afternoon Mr. W. had his revenge, He spoke to all three boys individually and got them to surrender to Christ, each without the other knowing.

"As I was going out to play cricket [Charlie said], he caught me unawar es and asked, 'Are you a Christian?' I said, 'I am not what you call a Christian. I have believed on Jesus Christ since I was knee high. Of course, I believe in the Church, too.' I thought, by answering him pretty close, I would get rid of him; but he stuck as tight as wax and said, 'Look here, "God so loved the world that He gave His only begotten son, that whosoever believeth in Him should not perish, but have everlasting life." 'You believe Jesus Christ died?' 'Yes' Do you believe the other half of the verse– "shall have everlasting life"?' 'No,' I said, 'I don't believe that,' He said, 'Now, don't you see that your statement contradicts God Either God or you is not speaking the truth, for you contradict one another. Which is it? Do you think that God is a liar?' 'No,' I said.

'Well, then aren't you inconsistent, believing one half of the verse and not the other half?' 'I suppose I am.' 'Well,' he said, 'Are you always going to be inconsistent? 'No,' I said, 'I suppose not always.' He said, 'Will you be consistent now?' I saw that I was cornered and I began to think, if I go out of this room inconsistent I won't carry very much self–respect. So I said, 'Yes, I will be consistent.'

'Well, don't you see that eternal life is a gift? When someone gives you a present at Christmas, what do you do? 'I take it and say "thank you." He said, 'will you say "thank you" to God for this gift?' Then I got down on my knees and I did say 'thank you' to God. And right then and there joy and peace came into my soul. I knew then what it was to be 'born again,' and the Bible, which had been so dry to me before, became everything."

Charlie said nothing to his brothers at the time, but on returning to Eton he wrote and told his father. Then a few days later at breakfast in their room at Eton, he and his brothers received a joint letter from their father saying how glad he was to hear the good news. They got a big surprise as they passed the letter from one to the other and found that the three brothers had each made his decision on the same day. So the "milksop," who was no good at games, was really an expert at the greatest game of all–catching men for Christ, and he had hooked three shy fish, all members of the Eton XI, in one day.

CHAPTER III

AN ALL-ENGLAND CRICKETER

CHARLIE was one of those boys who goes all out for the thing he loves. He was tremendously keen on cricket, and he was determined to do well at it. Upstairs in his bedroom at home there was a big wardrobe with a long glass. In front of it was a carpet with a seam down the centre. The way he argued to himself was this: If a man puts a dead straight bat every time in front of the ball, it must be impossible for the ball to hit the wicket. So he made it his first business to learn to play with a straight bat. Hour after hour he practiced in front of that lookingglass, keeping his bat along the seam of the carpet. He used to be ragged for taking things so seriously, but he stuck to it.

Another dodge of his a little later on was to make sure that he had his eye in for the first ball he had to play. If he was next man, he would sit on the edge of the ground with his eyes glued to a spot on the grass about 22 yards in front, so as to have his eye exactly accustomed to the length of the pitch from the moment he was at the wicket. He never smoked, and would not even remain in the dining–room after dinner, lest the smoke should affect his eye.

The three brothers, who were commonly known by their initials, J.E.K. (Kynaston), G.B. (George), and C.T. (Charlie), were only together one year in the Eton XI. They made one notable score, in the match against Winchester, whom they beat by an innings. In Eton's first innings J.E.K. made 52, C.T. 53 and G.B. 54! Eton also beat Harrow that year.

While the three brothers were together, they started a Bible Class. It was attended by several other boys, some of whom became well–known Christians later on, such as Colonel Granville –Smith of the Coldstream Guards, and a former Bishop of Madras

C.T. remained two more years at Eton, captaining the XI in his last year. They were lean years for Eton cricket, being beaten once by Harrow and drawing once; but this fact only made C.T's form stand out all the more. Thus the report of the Eton–Harrow match of 1879 said: "Incomparably the best cricketer was the Eton Captain, C.T. Studd. He should make a great name some day." Another report placed him, together with C.F.H. Leslie, the Rugby Captain, as the best all round Public School player of that year.

Before he left he also distinguished himself at racquets and fives:

"The final match for the singles Racquets came off on Monday [wrote the *Eton Chronicle*] in the presence of a densely crowded and exceedingly noisy gallery. Eastwood was generally the favourite, though Studd's form in the preceding match had made it pretty certain that he would not be easily beaten. As it happened he won with comparative case. We heartily congratulate him on his victory, which, considering his comparative inexperience of the game, was a very striking performance."

Later with J.D. Cobbold he represented Eton in the Public Schools Racquets Challenge Cup. They reached the final, where they were beaten by Rugby by four games to three, there being a difference of only one in the total aces, 88 against 87. C.T. also won the Eton House Fives.

When leaving, his housemaster, Mr. Cameron, wrote of him:

"Perhaps he might have done more in work, but it is hard for the Captain of the XI, and he has done no little good to all who have come under his influence. I think the secret of the charm of his character is that he thinks for others rather than for himself. We shall miss him terribly and it is sad parting."

Charlie's own comment was that he learnt a great deal more through cricket than through books!

He went up to Trinity College, Cambridge. As a Freshman he was given his Cricket Blue, and he made 52 in the second innings of the 'Varsity Match. The next year the three brothers were together in the 'Varsity XI, and C.T. began to fulfil the promise of the brilliant future which had been prophesied of him. He not only played for the 'Varsity, being second in the batting averages with an average of 42 and third in the bowling with an average of 16, but he also played for the Gentlemen v. Players.

Lillywhite's Cricket Record for the year said: "Very few players have a finer style: brilliant leg hitting and driving, with a very hard wrist stroke in front of point, a real straight bat, and a resolute nerve make together a batsman whose back bowlers are very glad to see."

It is interesting to note that his bats were specially made with the handles one inch longer than most. His wrists were so strong that he could manage the extra weight.

In one match, Cambridge v. The Gentlemen of England, J.E.K. and C.T. made 267 out of 362 runs, the former scoring 154, the latter 113. In another match the three brothers made 249 out of a total score of 504.

But it was in 1882 that C.T. reached the height of his fo rm. Tho ugh only a third-year man at the University, he rose to the very top of the cricket world, amateur and professional alike. It is doubtful whether any other undergraduate in the history of cricket has done such a thing. *Lillywhite's Annual* said that year:

"Mr. C.T. Studd must be given the premier position amongst the batsman of 1882, and it would be difficult to instance three finer innings played by so young a cricketer against the best bowling of the day than his threefigure scores against Australia and the players."

In the three matches referred to he made 118 v. Australia, 100 for the Gentlemen v. Players at Lord's and 126 not out *v*. The Gentlemen of England.

In bowling, only one in all England, a professional, Peate, had taken more wickets, and was ranked before him.

Only two matches of the year can be referred to in detail. Both created a sensation. The Australians were paying their third visit to England and had never yet beaten them; but this year they had sent over a very strong team, which included such famous players as Murdoch, Massie, Boyle, and the "Demon Bowler" Spofforth, whom some think the greatest bowler there has ever been.

G. B. Studd was Captain of Cambridge that year, and when the Australians asked that a match should be arranged with the University, he readily agreed. The President of the Club, an old Cambridge Don, cricketer and clergyman, was very indignant at the idea, for he thought, as most people did, that the University would get a sound beating and disgrace themselves. G.B's reply was that it would not matter anyhow, as everybody expected that result. So the match was arranged. The Australians were an unbeaten side when they came to Cambridge.

"The weather was all that could be desired and there was a larger attendance than ever seen before at the University ground. When Murdoch won the toss, I heard one or two people say, 'Cambridge are in for a day's outing,' and so most people thought. Bannerman and Massie began the Australian innings to the bowling of C.T. Studd and Ramsay. At starting runs came at the great pace, Massie drove Studd three times for four and Ramsay twice. Then, just as he had begun to look dangerous, he failed to get quite hold of a ball from Studd and was neatly caught at third man."

Then followed a quick and surprising collapse, ending in the whole side being out for 139, C.T. taking five wickets for 64 and Ramsay the other five J.E.K. and G.B. began the Cambridge innings. J.E.K. was soon out and three wickets were down for 55.

"C.T. then joined his brother and commenced a most remarkable innings. The cricket while the brothers were together was admirable. At 89 Spofforth clean bowled G.B. for a brilliant but somewhat lucky innings of 42. Bather now became C.T.'s partner and a most determined resistance was offered to the Australian bowling. The 100 went up amidst cheers, and then Studd made a splendid on–drive for four, the ball almost pitching on the ring. Runs were put on very rapidly, and there was a perfect roar of applause when the Australians' total was passed. The bowling was several times changed without effect. Studd continued to bat in grand form and scored an enormous majority of the runs. No parting was effected up to the call of time, the score being 187 for four wickets. C.T. was not out 85 and Bather 20. Of course, Studd's success was immensely popular, and he thoroughly deserved the enthusiastic reception which greeted him. Better and cleaner off driving has seldom been my lot to witness.

"Play was resumed on Tuesday. The attendance was, if anything, larger than on Monday. Excursion trains had been run down from London and other places, and these brought a lot of people to the match.

Bather was soon bowled, and Spencer; then Henry joined Studd, who completed his 100 amidst enthusiastic cheering. The old Etonian then hit Spofforth twice and four. With one run added, Studd was given out, caught at the wicket, and his long and wonderful innings came to a close. I have always had a high opinion of Studd, but I must say I never thought him capable of such a great performance. Playing against bowling that was quite new to him, he never seemed at a loss to know what to do with it, and was never in any way nervous."

The side was out for 266. This was followed by a second innings of 290 by the Australians, leaving the University 168 to make to win.

"Opinions were greatly divided as to whether or not the runs would be obtained. The brothers J.E.K. and G.B. were the first pair of batsmen. Both men played in fine form in starting, and the score rose rapidly. There were loud cheers as each ten appeared on the board. When the 100 went up there was a tumult of applause. G.B. was then out. For these two young cricketers to put on 106 runs for the first wicket was a great performance and will long be remembered by lovers of cricket, as it practically won the match for Cambridge. C. T. later made the winning hit, scoring 15 not out, Cambridge thus beating Australia by six wickets."

When Horan, one of the Australian team, had arrived at Cambridge for the match, he had said, "I hear they have a set of Studds in the Eleven," and later he added, "We shall win if we can get them Studds out." And he was right. They didn't!

Incidentally it was *Punch* who gave them the nick name "The set of Studds," and there was a banker who went one better than *Punch*. He had three gold studs for his evening–dress shirt engraved with the initials of the three brothers. Whichever made top score any day when all three were playing, went top in the shirt that night.

This match made C.T.'s name. Before the season ended he had added another century against the Australians, making two of the only three centuries scored against them that season. For it must be remembered that centuries were much rarer in those days when pitches were less perfect.

That year, with the three brothers playing, Cambridge also beat Lancashire, the champion country, and Oxford. Against Lancashire C.T. "showed by far the best batting in the match," scoring 69 and 38. The finish was most exciting, Lancashire, with five wickets to go down, wanting only 22 runs to win. Thanks, however, to capital bowling and fielding, these five wickets fell for 7 runs. Four of the five wickets were taken by C. T. Against Oxford, who were beat en by s even wickets , G. B. made top score in the first innings with a brilliant 120, and C.T. top score in the second with 69. In their second innings Oxford foolishly took chances with G.B. fielding at midoff, and as a consequence had three men run out. He was the finest mid–off of his day.

The other sensation of the season was the historic Test Match when Australia beat England for the first time, and when the term Ashes came into existence. A few days after the match the "*Sporting Times*" published the following epitaph:

"In Affectionate Remembrance
of
English Cricket,
Which died at the Oval on
29th August, 1882,
Deeply lamented by a large circle of
Sorrowing Friends and Acquaintances
R.I.P.
N.B.—The body will be cremated and
the ashes taken to Australia."

C.T. was a member of the English XI, which a wellknown critic thinks as good as any England has ever put in the field. The other members of the team were W.G. Grace, R.G. Barlow, G. Ulyett, A. P. Lucas, Hon. A. Lyttelton, J.M. Read, W. Barnes, A.G. Steel, A.N. Hornby (Captain), E. Peate. The match was watched at the Oval by a record crowd of over 20,000.

During the Australians' first innings, C.T. ran one of them out by a very smart piece of fielding. The ball was hit between Hornby and himself at extra cover and coverpoint. Hornby ran after the ball and C.T. ran after him, knowing that Hornby could not throw. The batsman, seeing it was Hornby and knowing that he could not throw, called for another run; Hornby picked up the ball, jerked it to C.T., who threw and ran the Australian out.

It seemed a certainty that England would win, for she had only 85 left to make in the last innings, and 50 went up with only 2 wickets down. Then came the collapse.

C.T.'s own account of the end of the match was as follows:

"The weather was cold. We sat in the Committee Room, and the windows were shut because of the cold. Except that such strange things happen in cricket, none dreamed we should be beaten.

"We had made over fifty for two wickets (there were less than ninety required to win when our innings began); everything was over, as they say, bar the shouting; runs had come freely enough. Then came the time when the best English batsmen played over after over and never made a run. If I remember right, something like eighteen to twenty overs were bowled without a run, maiden after maiden. They got out, and Hornby on his own account began to alter the order of going in. He asked me if I minded and I said, 'No.' Then things began to change and a procession began. Of course Hornby told me he was holding me in reserve. So I went in 8th and saw two wickets fall and myself never received a ball."

C.T. was joined by Peate for the last wicket. Peate, who was no batsman, had been warned to be careful and leave the run-getting to Studd, but after hitting a 2, he lashed out at a straight one from Boyle and was bowled. Afterwards when asked why he had done so, he made the famous witticism, "I could not trust Studd!" Australia won the match by 8 runs.

That winter C.T. was invited to go with the Test Team to Australia under the leadership of the Hon. Ivo Bligh, afterwards Lord Darnley, who remained his life long friend. *Punch* called him "St. Ivo," and said that he was setting out on a Pilgrimage to Australia to recover the Ashes. During the tour three matches were played against Australia, out of which England won two. After the third match, some Melbourne ladies put some Ashes into a small silver urn and gave them to Mr. Bligh. The urn had on it the following inscription:

When Ivo goes back with the Urn, the Urn,
Studds, Steel, Read and Tylecote return, return!
    The welkin will ring loud,
    The great crowd will feel proud
Seeing Barlow and Bates with the Urn, the Urn
And the rest coming home with the Urn.

This was the origin of the historic Ashes.

C.T. returned to captain Cambridge in his last year, 1883. Once again he was reckoned the leading all round player in England, the *Cricketing Annual* saying:

"Mr. C.T. Studd must for the second year in succession be accorded the premier position as an allround cricketer, and some years have elapsed since the post has been filled by a player so excellent in all the three departments of the game. His batting especially has been of the highest class." His Cambridge career has been described as "one long blaze of cricketing glory." In his last year he topped both bowling and batting average with 41.84 in batting and 14.65 in bowling. Indeed, through the previous ha lf century of University cricket only four batsmen had a better batting average, and only four a better bowling. A truly amazing record of all round brilliancy, and one which ranks him as one of the greatest all–round players that the game has produced.

He also won the Cambridge single Racquets Match and represented Cambridge against Oxford. He was beaten by C.F.H. Leslie. He took his B.A degree and came down from Cambridge in 1884.

Let it be carefully noted that C.T. was not just a "born cricketer," nor was cricket to him just a pastime to wile away spare hours. He made a serious business of it, and he set himself to get to the top of the tree at cricket as thoroughly as the scholar sets himself to get a first class in his Tripos. C.T. never regretted that he played cricket (although he regretted that he had allowed it to become an idol), for by applying himself to the game he learned lessons of courage, self–denial and endurance, which, after his life had been fully consecrated to Christ, were used in His service. The man who went all out to be an expert cricket player, later went all out to glorify his Saviour and extend His Kingdom.

CHAPTER IV

THE CRISIS

THE three brothers created a record at Cambridge which has never been equaled, by each being Captain of the XI in succession, G.B. in 82, C.T. in 83, and J.E.K. in 84. But the only one of the three who was outstanding as a witness for the Lord Jesus Christ as well as a cricketer, was J.E.K. Years after C.T. wrote to him from the heart of Africa:

"I never forget the influence your life had upon me, and how I admired your courage and loyalty to the Lord Jesus Christ, which earned for you that greatest of all compliments, for you remember our cricketing friends used to call you 'The Austere Man,' because your life was true on God, and you were true to them; for you were ever faithful in speaking to them about their souls."

When Captain of the XI, J.E.K. had organized and been Chairman of the remarkable Moody Mission, probably the most

MR. AND MRS. EDWARD STUDD
PARENTS OF C.T.

fruitful ever held in the University, which started by a group of men publicly mocking Moody from the front row of the audience and ended by their apology and the lasting conversion of some of them and a number of others.

But it was very different with C.T. For six years he had been a backslider. He gave the reason himself:

"Instead of going and telling others of the love of Christ, I was selfish and kept the knowledge to myself. The result was that gradually my love began to grow cold, and the love of the world began to come in. I spent six years in that unhappy backslidden state."

But as he rose to prominence in the cricket world, and especially while touring with the Test Team in Australia, there were two old ladies who set themselves to pray that he would be

"Esteeming the reproach of Christ greater riches than the treasures in Egypt"

TEDWORTH HOUSE, WILTSHIRE, THE HOME OF C. T.'S BOYHOOD
(Inset: C.T. in the heart of Africa in later years)

brought back to God. The answer came suddenly. His brother G.B., to whom he was especially attached, was thought to be dying. C.T. was constantly at his bedside, and whilst sitting there, watching as he hovered between life and death, these thoughts came welling up in his mind, "Now what is all the popularity of the world worth to George? What is all the fame and flattery worth? What is it worth to possess all the riches in the world, when a man comes to face Eternity?" And a voice seemed to answer, "Vanity of vanities, all is vanity."

"All those things [he said] had become as nothing to my brother. He only cared about the Bible and the Lord Jesus Christ, and God taught me the same lesson. In His love and goodness, He restored my brother to health, and as soon as I could get away I went to hear Mr. Moody. There the Lord met me again and restored to me the joy of His salvation. Still further, and what was better than all, He set me to work for Him, and I began to try and persuade my friends to read the Gospel, and to speak to them individually about their souls.

"I cannot tell you what joy it gave me to bring the first soul to the Lord Jesus Christ. I have tasted almost all the pleasures that this world can give. I do not suppose there is one that I have not experienced, but I can tell you that those pleasures were as nothing compared to the joy that the saving of that one soul gave me. I went on working for some time, and then the cricket season came round, and I thought I must go into the cricket field and get the men there to know the Lord Jesus. Formerly I had as much love for cricket as any man could have, but when the Lord Jesus came into my heart, I found that I had something infinitely better than cricket. My heart was no longer in the game; I wanted to win souls for the Lord. I knew that cricket would not last, and honour would not last, and nothing in this world would last, but it was worthwhile living for the world to come. During those meeting one of my sincerest friends was brought to know that his sins were forgiven."

He got several of the England XI to go and hear Moody, including A.G. Steel, and the Captain of the Test Team, Ivo Bligh. Bligh wrote to him afterwards, "An address from that man goes right home, and makes one think more than any man I have yet heard. He is so thoroughly practical. I hope to see you next week at the Oval. Mind you make a long score, there's a good old boy." Years later Bligh wrote and told C.T. how he daily prayed for him, and that he was trusting the Saviour; likewise Alan Steel. But of all his cricketing friends, the one with whom he had maintained the closest link has been A.J. Webbe of Oxford and England fame, now a member of the M.C.C. Committee.

There was another too, whose life was changed in these meetings, whose name was destined to become a household word, Sir Wilfred Grenfell of Labrador. He was a medical student at the time, and went to hear Moody, and this was his own account of it :

"It was so new to me that when a tedious prayer bore began with a long oration, I started to leave. Suddenly the leader, who afterwards I discovered was D.L. Moody, called out to the audience, 'Let us sing a hymn while our brother finishes his prayer.' His practicality interested me and I stayed the service out.

"Later I went to hear the brothers J.E.K. and C.T. Studd speak at some subsidiary meeting of the Moody campaign. They were natural athletes, and I felt I could listen to them. Never shall I forget that meeting of the Studd brothers, the audience being asked to stand up if they intended to try to follow Christ. It appeared a very sensible question to me, but I was amazed how hard I found it to stand up. At last one boy out of a hundred or more, in sailor rig, from an Industrial or Reformatory ship on the Thames, suddenly rose. It seemed to me such a wonderfully courageous act, for I knew perfectly what it would mean to him, that I immediately found myself on my feet, and went out feeling that I had crossed the Rubicon and must do something to prove it."

The Moody Mission came to an end.

"Mr. Moody left for America [continued C.T.] and then I wanted to know what my life's work for the Lord Jesus Christ was to be. I wanted only to serve Him, and I prayed God to show me. But here I made another mistake; for instead of trusting entirely to God to show me, I went to my friends. Thus I tried to find out the Lord's guidance by common sense; and instead of getting into the light, I got into darkness. I became very restless and anxious, my health gave way, and I had to go into the country to recuperate.

"Having spent three months in reading my Bible and praying to God for guidance, I came back much better, but still not knowing what I was to do. I decided to read for the Bar until He should show me.

I found, however, when I got back to Town, that it was absolutely impossible for me conscientiously to go into any business or profession. It seemed so thoroughly inconsistent. God had given me far more than was sufficient to keep my body and soul together, and, I thought, how could I spend the best years of my life in working for myself and the honours and pleasures of this world, while thousands and thousands of souls are perishing every day without having heard of Christ?

"About this time I met with a tract written by an atheist. It read as follows : 'Did I firmly believe, as millions say they do, that the knowledge and practice of religion in this life influences destiny in another, religion would mean to me everything. I would cast away earthly enjoyments as dross, earthly cares as follies, and earthly thoughts and feelings as vanity. Religion would be my first waking thought, and my last image before sleep sank me into unconsciousness. I should labour in its cause alone. I would take thought for the morrow of Eternity alone. I would esteem one soul gained for heaven worth a life of suffering. Earthly consequences should never stay my hand, nor seal my lips. Earth, its joys and its griefs, would occupy no moment of my thoughts. I would strive to look upon Eternity alone, and on the Immortal Souls around me, soon to be everlastingly happy or everlastingly miserable. I would go forth to the world and preach to it in season and out of season, and my text would be, WHAT SHALL IT PROFIT A MAN IF HE GAIN THE WHOLE WORLD AND LOSE HIS OWN SOUL?' I at once saw that this was the truly consistent Christian life. When I looked back upon my own life I saw how inconsistent it had been. I therefore determined that from that time forth my life should be consistent, and I set myself to know what was God's will for me. But this time I determined not to consult with flesh and blood, but just wait until God should show me."

The vision of souls had gripped C.T. and was to grip him still more; but he had yet another lesson to learn of infinite importance for his future work–that mere zeal would never make him a successful worker for Christ. He must have *power*. "Ye shall receive power··· and ye shall be witnesses unto Me." The consequence was, as we shall see, that when he definitely set himself to seek and find God's plan for his life, the first answer God gave was a revelation of his own need, and the next that this need could be supplied by receiving the fullness of the Holy Ghost. As soon as C.T. saw this in the Scriptures, he received the Holy Ghost like a little child, by a simple act of complete surrender and faith. He was then divinely equipped to receive and obey the call, and to go through the tests that followed. In a few days it came:

"About three days afterwards a great friend of mine came back to Town, and asked me to go to a Bible meeting with him. I went, and after we had read the Bible for some time, and spoken about it among ourselves, he said, 'Have you heard of the extraordinary blessing Mrs. W. has received?' 'No.' 'Well, you know she has been an earnest Christian worker nearly her whole life, and she has had a good deal of sorrow and trouble, which has naturally influenced and weighed upon her. But lately somehow God has given her such a blessing that it does not affect her at all now. Nothing, in fact, seems to trouble her. She lives a life of perfect peace. Her life is like one of heaven upon earth.' We began at once looking into the Bible to see if God had promised such a blessing as this, and it was not long before we found that God had promised it to believers, a peace which passes all understanding, and a joy that is unspeakable. We then began to examine ourselves earnestly, and we found that we had not got this. But we wanted the best thing that God could give us, so we knelt down and asked Him to give us this blessing. Then we separated.

"I was very much in earnest about it, so when I went up to my own room I again asked God to give me this peace and joy. That very day I met with the book, *The Christian's Secret of a Happy Life*. In it was stated that this blessing is exactly what God gives to everyone who is ready and willing to receive it. I found that the reason why I had not received it was just this, that I had not made room for it, and I found, as I sat there alone thinking, that I had been keeping back from God what belonged to Him. I found that I had been bought with the price of the precious blood of the Lord Jesus, and that I had kept back myself from Him, and had not wholly yielded.

"As soon as I found this out, I went down on my knees and gave myself up to God in the words of Frances Ridley Havergal's Consecration Hymn:

"Take my life and let it be,
Consecrated, Lord, to thee.

"I found the next step was to have simple, childlike faith, to believe that what I had committed to God, He was also willing to take and keep. I knew I had committed my soul to His keeping and He was able to keep that; how much more then was He able to keep me and what belonged to me in this world? I realized that my life was to be one of simple, childlike faith, and that my part was to trust, not to do. I was to trust in Him and He would work in me to do His good pleasure. From that time my life has been different, and He has given me that peace that passes understanding and that joy which is unspeakable.

"It was not very long before God led me to go to China. I had never thought of going out of the country before. I had felt that England was big enough for me. But now my mind seemed constantly to run in the direction of the Lord's work abroad. I went one day with my friend Mr. Stanley Smith to Mr. Mc.Carthy's farewell, and I shall never forget the earnest workers to preach the Gospel. I thought, however, that I would not decide at once, because people would say I was led by impulse. I therefore resolved that after the meeting I would go and ask God. I prayed to God to guide me by His word. I felt that there was one thing alone which could keep me from going, and that was the love of my mother; but I read that passage, "He that loves father or mother more than Me is not worthy of Me,' after which I knew it was God's will, and I decided to go."

Then came the big test. He met with the strongest opposition from his own family. It had been shock enough to the whole family circle when his father had been converted, but that one of them should become a missionary was the last straw. Every persuasion was used, even to the extent of bringing in Christian workers to dissuade him. Even a relation, whose witness had been a great blessing to him, said to him one evening, "Charlie, I t hink you are making a great mistake. You are away every night at the meetings and you do not see your mother. I see her, and this is just breaking her heart. I think you are wrong." But C.T. was not again to be moved by human advice.

"I said, 'Let us ask God. I don't want to be pig headed and go out there of my own accord. I just want to do God's will.' It was hard to have this one, who had been such a help, think it was a mistake. We got down on our knees and put the whole matter in God's hands. That night I could not get to sleep, but it seemed as though I heard someone say these words over and over, 'Ask of Me and I will give thee the heathen for thine inheritance, and the uttermost parts of the earth for thy possession.' I knew it was God's voice speaking to me, and that I had received my marching orders to go to China."

Many said that he was making a huge mistake to go and bury himself in the interior of China. They pointed out the influence which he would have with the young men of England. The devil must have used a very similar argument to Moses, "What an influence you will have, if you stay in the palace"; but Moses went God's way, renounced all, went into exile, and became the Saviour of the nation. C.T. did the same, and the first–fruits of that act, so far from being the exerting of some vague influence, was the bursting forth of a Holy Ghost revival among students, the like of which has never been seen before or since, and which reached on to every University in the English speaking world. How many fail at this point. God calls along some lonely path, but "my people are against it." How few go through with the single eye. Thank God, even "the tears and beseeching of a devoted, loving mother" would not move C.T. In the agony of the conflict, when he was almost wavering, he received one last word from God which finally settled the matter. He was standing on a station platform at night under the flickering light of the lamp, and in desperation asked God to give him a message. He took out his Testament, opened it and read, "A man's foes shall be they of his own household." From that moment he never looked back.

CHAPTER V

A REVIVAL BREAKS OUT AMONG STUDENTS

HAVING made the decision, he had an interview with Mr. Hudson Taylor, the Director of the China Inland Mission, and was accepted as an associate member of the C.I.M. His friend, Stanley P. Smith, the stroke oar of the Cambridge Boat, had also received the call, and applied. In a few weeks five more young men had joined them. Someone gave them the name of the "Cambridge Seven," and in a short time the whole Press, religious and secular alike, were broadcasting the news that seven young men were going out to China as missionaries, including no less leading lights in the athletic world than an all–England cricketer, the stroke of the Cambridge Boat, the stroke oar of one of the trial eights, a Dragoon guardsman, and an officer of the Royal Artillery. In the history of missions no band of volunteers has caught the imagination of the public as these seven, and their going gave a new impetus to the whole cause. Her majesty Queen Victoria was pleased to receive a booklet giving their testimonies.

Then began the blessing among students. Studd and Stanley Smith were asked to go up to a student gathering in Edinburgh. The invitation came from some of the leading professors in the University who were keen Christian–Professors Henry Drummond, Cairns, Greenfield, etc. The organization of the meeting had been under taken by a group of medical students, one of whom writes:

"We resolved to do Christ's work in every detail in the best possible style. To this end, we asked the University Printers to have our notices printed on good paper, and in good taste. All our hymns were carefully chosen and well printed and each hymn sheet had the University Crest embossed upon it. We hoped that the students would take them home and keep them. We hired the Free Assembly Hall, because we expected a crowd. We decided students only should be admitted, and put it at the bottom of our notices.

"For several days before the meeting we had a number of sandwich man with large posters walking in the neighbourhood of the University and Infirmary. We had committed ourselves to great things. Our prayers were answered far above our asking. Twenty minutes before the appointed hour men were rushing up the steps of the Assembly Hall, asking if there was room (some of them were honours men).

"Studd and Stanley Smith had arrived at lunch time and spent the afternoon in their host's drawing–room in prayer till they got victory. Nearly all the gentlemen invited came, and before they went into the Hall they all knelt in prayer for God's blessing. Studd finished by *thanking God for the result !* Meanwhile, the students in the Hall had been singing their usual before–lecture songs and beating time with their sticks.

"As soon as Studd and Stanley Smith entered, they were loudly cheered. We had made it plain on our notices that they were going to China as missionaries, and our men had come to hear what Studd, who had made the biggest score at cricket in Cambridge, had to say about religion. They admired their consecration. Again and again during their addresses they were cheered. Stanley Smith was eloquent, but Studd couldn't speak a bit–it was the fact of his devotion to Christ which told, and he, if anything, made the greatest impression. Professor Charteris was in the chair, and he announced that if any would like to shake hands with them and wish them God–speed, they could come forward as soon as the Benediction had been pronounced. All the men there were students, and we wondered who would have the courage to do so, but no sooner had the Benediction been pronounced, than there was a stampede for the platform. A great impression had been made, and they were crowding round Studd and Smith to hear more about Christ; deep earnestness was written on the faces of many. A great religious movement had its births, and it was all so evidently the work of the Holy Spirit of God. Many of those students were our best men. We were now face to face with the challenge; we were bound to go on; we could not possibly stop. All felt that we must have these two Cambridge students back before they left for China. I remember Professor Greenfield (who was the President of the Medical Students' Association that year), Coming to me and urging that we try and get them back. They were leaving for London by the 10.30 express. We walked down with Studd, and when we got to the Waverley Station platform, we found that a number of students had gone down to see them off. As soon as they caught sight of Studd, there was a cry of 'Speech,' and Studd had to stand on one of the seats and address them still further. We overheard a gentleman asking a porter, 'Who are these?' The porter replied in Scotch Doric, "*Th're medical students, but th're off their heeds.*' As the train moved off, some ran up to the end of the platform, cheering. So ended the first students' meeting."

They consented to return, and accordingly a meeting was arranged in the large U.P. Hall. Admission was limited to students, and when the hour had arrived, over 2,000 had assembled. Professor Charteris was in the chair and many of the leading ministers and professors of the University occupied the platform. One of them, Doctor D.A. Moxey, wrote afterwards :

"A wonderful work of grace has begun, and is going on, in our University. The event that has precipitated the shower of blessing which has, and is, falling in our midst is the recent visit of two young Christian athletes from Cambridge, who are now on their way to preach Christ to the Chinese. Students, like other young men, are apt to regard professedly religious men of their own age as wanting in manliness, unfit for the river or cricket field, and only good for Psalm–singing and pulling a long face, but the big, muscular hands and the long arms of the excaptain of the Cambridge Eight, stretched out in entreaty while he eloquently told out the story of Redeeming Love, capsized their theory; and when Mr. C.T. Studd, a name to them familiar as a household word, and perhaps the greatest gentleman bowler in England, supplemented his brother athlete's words by quiet but intense and burning utterances of personal testimony to the love and power of a personal Saviour, opposition and criticism were alike disarmed, and professors and students together were seen in tears, to be followed in the after meeting by the glorious sight of professors dealing with students, and students with one another.

"We returned to a marvellous time [wrote C.T.]. All day long men were coming for interviews restricted to a quarter of an hour, which consisted of 'Well, are you a Christian?' 'No.' 'Would you like to be one?' 'Yes.' 'Well, let us pray,' and the fellow would get up full of joy–he'd got Salvation. Then bands of these fellows were formed under good leaders and went all over the Universities of England, Scotland and Ireland spreading the fire.

"When we went round the students, we were in a mortal funk about meeting them, because we had never done anything like this. So we used to stay sometimes all night by the fire on the mat, sometimes praying and sometimes sleeping. In one house our host said in the morning, 'Oh, you should not bother to make your beds!' "

In company with Mr. Reginald Radcliffe, Studd and Stanley Smith then took an evangelistic tour and visited many of the large cities. The interest manifested was extraordinary. Young men especially came in large numbers to see and hear them.

"We had a grand meeting at Rochdale [C.T. wrote to his mother on January 28, 1885]. They say there had never been such a meeting there before. The hall was crammed. We had a huge after–meeting. It was like a charge of dynamite exploded among them.
"[Again] Splendid news from Liverpool. The fire is still burning and over sixty professed conversion on that one night. I cannot tell how very much the Lord has blessed us, and we daily grow in the knowledge of Jesus and His wonderful love; what a different life from my former one; why, cricket and racquets and shooting are nothing to this overwhelming joy. Finding out so much about not

only the needs of the heathen, but also of the poor in London and all great towns has increased my horror at the luxurious way I have been living; so many suits and clothes of all sorts, whilst thousands are starving and perishing of cold, so all must be sold when I come home if they have not been so before. Mother dear, I do pray God to show you that it is such a privilege to give up a child to be used of God to saving poor sinners who have never even heard of the name of Jesus. God bless you, dear darling mother, and I know He will do it, and turn your sorrow into joy."

At Leicester they met F.B. Meyer, who wrote later:

"The visit of Messrs. Stanley Smith and Studd to Melbourne Hall will always mark an epoch in my own life. Before then my Christian life had been spasmodic and fitful; now flaming up with enthusiasm, and then pacing wearily over leagues of grey ashes and cold cinders. I saw that these young men had something which I had not, but which was within them a constant source of rest and strength and joy. And never shall I forget a scene at 7 a.m. in the grey mist of a November morning, as daylight was flickering into the bedroom, paling the guttering candles, which from a very early hour had been lighting up the page of Scripture, and revealing the figures of the devoted Bible students, who wore the old cricket or boating blazer of earlier days, to render them less sensible to the raw, damp climate. The talk we had then was one of the formative influences of my life. 'You have been up early,' I said to Charlie Studd. 'Yes,' said he, 'I got up at four o'clock this morning. Christ always knows when I have had sleep enough, and He wakes me to have a good time with Him.' I asked, 'What have you been doing this morning?' And he replied, 'You know that the Lord says, "If ye love Me, keep my commandments"; and I was just looking through all the commandments that I could find that the Lord gave, and putting a tick against them if I have kept them, because I do love Him.' 'Well,' I inquired, 'How can I be like you?' He replied, 'Have you ever given yourself to Christ, for Christ to fill you?' 'Yes,' I said, 'I have done so in a general way, but I don't know that I have done it particularly.' He answered, 'You must do it particularly also.' I knelt down that night, and thought I could give myself to Christ as easily as possible. I gave Him an iron ring, the iron ring of my will, with all the keys of my life on it, except one little key that I kept back. And the Master said, 'Are they all here?' I said, 'They are all there but one, the key of a tiny closet in my heart, of which I must keep control.' He said, 'If you don't trust Me in all, you don't trust Me at all.' I tried to make terms; I said, 'Lord, I will be so devoted in everything else, but I can't live without the contents of that closet.' I believe that my whole life was just hovering in the balance, and if I had kept the key of that closet, and mistrusted Christ, He never would have trusted me with the ministry of his blessed Word. He seemed to be receding from me, and I called Him back and said, 'I am not willing, but I am willing to be made willing.' It seemed as though He came near and took that key out of my hand, and went straight for the closet. I knew what He would find there, and He knew too. Within a week from that time He had cleared it right out. But He filled it with something so much better! Why, what a fool I was! He wanted to take away the sham jewels, to give me the real ones. He just took away the thing which was eating out my life, and instead gave me Himself. Since then I have reckoned on Him to keep; but full consecration is a necessary condition of any deep experience of His keeping power."

The three great farewell meetings for the whole seven were

arranged by the C.I.M. in Cambridge, Oxford and London. No description can convey to those not present an adequate idea of the extraordinary character of those meetings. At Cambridge the meeting was one which, it is not too much to say, will be memorable in the history of the University. The following extracts from the letter of the Cambridge correspondent of *The Record* gave the testimony of an impartial witness :

"By far the most remarkable event of this week in our religious world has been the meeting of farewell to the China Inland missionaries in the large room at the Guild Hall. Soon after 7.30 p.m. the great hall was crowded in every corner–floor, orchestra and gallery. Quite twelve hundred persons must have been present, including a very large number of gownsmen. Professor Babington took the chair, and his presence there was a valuable testimonial of confidence in a devoted, spiritual enterprise on the part of a leading representative of science. One after another the new missionary volunteers spoke, with very different degrees of eloquence, but with beautifully uniform simplicity, stating their motive and hope, and confessing their Lord's Name and claims. It was, we can hardly doubt, the most remarkable missionary meeting held within living memory at Cambridge."

Even in the 'Varsity sermon reference was made to Studd's testimony by the Master of Pembroke, with the comment :

"What a victory is scored to faith, for, however eccentric his conduct may be thought, plainly he has demonstrated that there are unseen powers that sway a man's heart much more forcibly than any motives of the world."

At Oxford the vast area of the Corn Exchange, the largest building in the possession of the city, was full to overflowing.

The Exeter Hall meeting in London was an occasion never to be forgotten by those who were privileged to be present.

"Long before the time for beginning, the hall was so densely packed that it appeared to be a living mass of human beings. When Mr. George Williams came forward to occupy the chair, the sight was such as even Exeter Hall, with its long roll of religious gatherings, could hardly have paralleled. As each speaker related how he was led to accept Christ as a personal Saviour, and that through faith in the Lord Jesus religion had become to him a bright and living reality, the vast audience was deeply moved. Never before probably in the history of missions has so unique a band set out to labour in the foreign field. Students who have just completed their course at College, and have decided to devote themselves to foreign missionary work; veterans who have been home on furlough and are returning–these we are accustomed to seeing on such occasions. But when before were the stroke of a University eight, the Captain of a University XI, an Officer of the Royal Artillery, and an Officer of the Dragoon Guards, seen standing side by side renouncing the careers in which they had already gained no small distinction, putting aside the splendid prizes of earthly ambition, taking leave of the social circles in which they shone with no mean brilliance, and plunging into that warfare whose splendours are seen only by faith, and whose rewards seem so shadowy to the unopened vision of ordinary men? It was a sight to stir the blood and a striking testimony to the power of the uplifted Christ to draw to Himself not the weak, the emotional, and the illiterate only, but all that is noblest in strength and finest in culture."

CHAPTER VI

C.T. BECOMES A CHINAMAN

THE Seven sailed in February, 1885. They had a lively time on boardship :

"When we got on board [wrote C.T. to his mother] there were seven second–class passengers, and we trust that all are now God's own children. The case of one is truly marvellous. The man is a Captain of an Indian steamer. He came home a few weeks ago, and has been noted for lying, drunkenness, swearing and blasphemy. Of course he is well known throughout the ship; the man who looked after the refrigerator said, 'Well, I do not believe in religion or conversion or miracles, but if the Captain is converted, then I will believe.' Well, thank God, He has brought even this man to know Jesus as his Saviour. He had looked forward to the time when we joined the ship, intending to have some rare fun with us and make us butts and laughingstocks. Hoste began to talk to him the first day, asking him if he ever read the Bible. He said, 'Oh yes, but I don't believe in it, I consider it all rot.' He read but only to scoff, and for three days he and Hoste read, but only with like results. Then somehow one afternoon the Lord led me to go and speak to him about his soul. I had not spoken to him previously, and he at once began with a host of freethinkers' arguments. I suppose we were talking for two hours, and for about an hour and a half it seemed hopeless; but the Lord led me to continue, and I told him of the happiness the Lord had given me, and he said, 'Well, you ought to be thankful, for many have been seeking for that for years and years with all their might, and have not obtained it.' I told him how it was simply trusting, and explained as simply as I could. Somehow his opposition and arguing seemed to have quite suddenly taken a turn, and he poured out his heart to me, all about his past life and the number of marvellous deliverances from death which he had had. He seemed softened and I urged him to decide at one, but he said it would be merely with the lips and not with his heart at present. So I said, 'Then don't, but just think it over,' and with a few more words I left him. He had told me he had left England after having quarreled with everybody he knew and without bidding either his brother or mother good-bye. What was my joy in the evening when a sailor came and told me that after I had spoken to him, he had gone down and written home for forgiveness. The Captain himself says he hardly knows why he did so, but he felt that he must. After doing this he felt relieved and thought he would act on what I said when I left him, and 'Ask and receive, that his joy might be full.' He just went down on his knees in his cabin and told the Lord Jesus that He had said that He had died for sinners, and that he was a sinner, and asked Him to receive and save him. The Lord heard and answered him, and he is rejoicing in fullness of heart. Hoste had some prayer with him next morning, which clinched the whole affair; and now he is just as active for the Lord Jesus as he was formerly for the devil. He has three times publicly given his testimony. His whole life is changed and most of his day taken up with reading the Bible. Praise the Lord, it is quite lovely, and has produced a profound impression throughout the ship. But not only have these been brought to the Lord, but also several of the stewards, and they say that the principal part of the conversation is about these things. You can imagine what a change that means among a ship's company."

Three months later, and their own mothers would hardly have recognised these seven young men! From officers and University graduates they changed to Chinese with pigtails, skirts and long-sleeved gowns complete, for according to the tenets of the C.I.M., they believed that the only way of reaching the Chinese of inland China was to become like them.

Another four months, and they were scattered far afield in inland China, Charlie going north to Pingyang and Taiyuen. Immense journeys by mule, foot and houseboat, ploughing through mud, sleeping in dirty Chinese inns, a month or two spent in this inland city and that, getting to grips with the language, and, above all, many days and hours spent in close communion with God and His Word–such were his first eighteen months of pioneering in China. The outstanding lesson which he learnt during this period was to become a man of one Book. From this time onward it became a principle of his life to read the Bible, almost to the exclusion of other books, marking it copiously, and receiving it in the attitude of a little child, in simple dependence upon the

Holy Spirit to illuminate the Word to him. Thus, living in direct communion with God through the Spirit and the Word, he never afterwards felt the need of Conventions or other help from man to sustain and guide his spiritual life. He had learned the secret of walking with God alone.

An extract or two from his letters to his mother gives an idea of his experiences. It is remarkable the joy he had under conditions which were such a total contrast to the comforts with which he had been surrounded in his beautiful home.

"Shanghai, April 1, 1885. The whole town has been talking of the meetings here, in fact, the Lord has turned it upside down. The Chaplain of the Cathedral's conversion and testimony has indeed been the explosion of a large charge of spiritual dynamite. He said publicly, 'Last night if the Lord had come I should have been a lost soul; but if the Lord comes tonight, I shall be a saved soul.'

"I have been laughing all day at our grotesque appearance. Stanley, Monty (Beauchamp), and A.P.T. (Arthur Polhill Turner) have been converted into Chinamen; we put on the clothes this morning, were duly shaved and pigtailed; the other three, notwithstanding advice to the contrary, had their moustaches off; it does make them look so funny, I cannot help roaring whenever I see them. Monty, Stanley and I make huge Chinamen; it makes us very conspicuous, as Chinamen are short. Stanley makes the best Chinamen. Monty is far too redfaced, and looks most comic."

He went as far as Hanchung with the two Polhill Turners, a distance of 1,800 miles by the Yangtse and Han Rivers, which took them three months.

"Hankow, April 22. We are moored alongside one another with crowds of boats on either side, so altogether it is a tight fit. I do wish you could see us sitting here. The inside of our boat consists of three rooms, two sleeping and one sitting. The sleeping rooms measure six feet long by seven feet broad and about five and a half feet high. They are very comfortable. No doubt one would not have thought so some time ago, but now they seem quite luxurious. This will D.V. be our home for about three months, and as we have a native teacher on board who cannot speak a word of English, we trust we shall be well advanced in the language by the time we reach Hanchung. It is so trying to be unable to speak one word; but oh, what joy it will be when I can, and how you will all share in that joy too, when the first convert comes."

"April 23. This is the first walk I have had in Chinese dress which even approached to comfort, for Chinese feet are small, whereas you know mine are large, and I could not get a pair of shoes large enough. The first shoemaker called in said he never had made such a pair as I wanted and fled from the house, utterly refusing to undertake such a gigantic operation. However, another was found; but when he brought them, he said that he had made many, many pairs of shoes for many years, but he had never made such a pair as these before. It is a great joke amongst the people, and the Chinamen often point and have a good laugh at them in the streets.

"It is terribly hot, but that is most enjoyable. These clothes are delicious for hot weather. I am now sitting writing to you in nothing but a pair of white calico pajamas enormously loose everywhere, and a white limp calico native shirt. When we go a walk we put on a blue thin calico gown something like a nightgown with very long loose sleeves. One does see the wisdom of bringing as few things as possible out here and using native things only."

"May 26. [He write s to his younger brothers Reggie and Bertie at Eton.] We were over–run with rats who during the night would take away our socks, nibbling off our legging tapes, taking away our blotting paper, and putting them at the bottom of the boat in their nest. They caused us a good deal of annoyance, so we thought of setting traps for them; but we decided not to do so, but simply to ask the Lord to rid us of the grievance. Since that time we have had no further trouble with them.

"···I do not say, Don't play games or cricket and so forth. By all means play and enjoy them, giving thanks to Jesus for them. Only take care that games do not become an idol to you, as they did to me. What good will it do to anybody in the next world to have been even the best player that ever has been? And then think of the difference between that and winning souls for Jesus. Oh! if you have never tasted the joy of leading one soul to Jesus, go and ask our Father to enable you to do so, and then you will know what real true joy is. The time is so short, such a little time to rescue souls from hell, for there will be no rescue work in heaven··· I have written earnestly because I know the joy there is in Jesus and because I well know the innumerable temptations you are exposed to in a Public School life."

From Hanchung he went northward to Pingyang–fu by land, where they were to meet Mr. Hudson Taylor, a distance of several weeks. It was a rough journey, during which he showed amazing endurance through great suffering.

"We slept very comfortably on the bare boards, it being hot. Up at 2 a.m. to have a read with a candle, got everything ready at 3:30 to start at 4. We had two nice bathes in the small river alongside the bank during the day. My feet got very sore.

"Next day my feet were so bad that I had to leave the boots off and take to sandals; but my skin not being made of leather like the coolies, the straw and string played havoc with me and as each step cut deeper, it was not all sugar for the 30 miles that day. Next day it was of course worse, and after I had gone 12 miles I had to take off the sandals and go bare foot. When I got in, my feet were in an awful state, seven raw places on the two feet; but, praise the Lord, it did make one appreciate one's rest in getting in. We generally walk eight miles before having breakfast, then we stop at an open shop or rather Chinese restaurant, consisting of a hovel with tables and forms and the cooking place, at which we get some rice. Oh! we do enjoy our meals on the road. I am now quite a Chinaman and enjoy the rice immensely, in fact, I prefer the Chinese to the foreign food.

"On Saturday my companions (two colporteurs), who were anxious to do the journey quickly, were bent on doing 40 miles. This was not a bright lookout for me with my feet. They wanted to get me a horse but could not. So bad were my feet that it seemed an impossibility to do such a distance; but the Lord did enable me, how I do not know; I know it was very painful indeed, and of course my feet got worse. Next day 38 miles. Euh! Each step was like a knife going into them, but I never felt the Lord's presence nearer the whole time. I was mostly alone, especially the last day, as I could not keep up with the others. But I do thank the Lord for it all, for He has taught me so many, many lessons by this suffering. One simply felt bursting with praise and wonder at how the Lord had enabled one to get there at all."

"Singan. Oct. 19. I know you will be anxious to hear how my foot is, so I will tell you how it got better. Though I rested it, it would not heal, but got very puffy and discharged a good deal. So I asked Hogg if he would anoint me with oil in the Name of the Lord, James v. 14 and 15, as I believed the Lord would heal my foot. He hesitated at first, but we read James v. together and prayed about it, and then he said he could see no reason against it, and did so. Since then my foot has got most rapidly better. Next day in faith I took it as being well (though it looked anything but so), and walked a good deal on it. It was much less swollen at night. I have continued to do nearly 20 miles a day on it since, with the result that it has lost all swelling and is as fine as the sound one and there is no discharge. I do praise the Lord for this."

"Pingyang. Nov. 3. Oh! mother, I can't describe the longing to speak about Jesus to these poor souls⋯."

"We have just been having a talk over Chinese hardships!!! and we want to know where they are, for we cannot find them and they are a myth. This is far the best life, so healthy and good, lots to eat and drink and good hard healthy beds, fine fresh air; and what else does a man want?"

"Pingyang, Feb. 7, 1886. [A first reference to one of the great secrets of his life–the early morning hours with God.] The Lord is so good and always gives me a large dose of Spiritual Champagne every morning which braces one up for the day and night. Of late I have had such glorious times. I generally wake about 3.30 a.m. and feel quite wide awake, so have a good read, etc., and then have an hour's sleep or so before finally getting up. I find what I read then is stamped indelibly on my mind all through the day: and it is the very quietest of times, not a foot astir, nor a sound to be heard, saving that of God. If I miss this time I feel like Samson shorn of his hair and so of all his strength. I see more and more how much

I have to learn of the Lord. I want to be a workman approved, not just with a 'pass' degree as it were. Oh! how I wish I had devoted my early life, my whole life to God and His word. How much have I lost by those years of self–pleasing and running after this world's honours and pleasures.

"What a life the Spirit lives out in us when He possesses us. It is so simple too: just to remember 'I *have been* crucified with Christ,' I am dead. 'It is no longer I that live, but Christ that liveth in me.' My part just to *let* Him live in me."

"May 8. [During a few months spent alone at Chin Wu, where he had gone to keep the station open, and jumped at the opportunity of being absolutely alone amongst the Chinese.] My way has been hedged in and all to give me this honeymoon time with the Lord; so quiet and as cool a place as anyone could wish for. My watch went wrong on my way down, and I sent it off to the coast, so here I am living regardless of hours, the sun being my only clock. I haven't an idea what time I get up or breakfast, all I know is the former is about sunrise, which is early here. We have Chinese prayers after breakfast, then I read for three or four hours with the Evangelist till lunch time, when I break off for about an hour for a little English reading, *The Christian* or Bible generally; then study again till about an hour before sundown, when I issue forth with tracts, Gospels and my Bible, and go into the country for a walk. I generally get a talk or two with some Chinese. This is my singing time too.

Then I have a cut off the joint (Bible) before my return. After tea, 'Friday' (my cook) and I read a portion together; then I have some more quiet reading on my own account and perhaps a slice of Chinese, and so, declaring His faithfulness every night, I hop joyfully on to my festive sleeping board. I have to restrain Friday's over zeal in cooking. He seems to think I ought to live like a 'tip-top' Mandarin. As it is I live royally, my day's food costs as much as 4d. a day. Friday is very curious; if I don't eat much breakfast he at once spots it and cooks three instead of two bowls of rice for lunch."

In July he went again to Tai–Yuen for a conference : "I was staying with Mr. Adamson of the Bible Society, Cassells was also there. Adamson sickened of what was thought to be Typhus Fever. Of course dear old Cassells and I were most ambitious to nurse him, but eventually with difficulty I gained the day and Cassells went off to another house. The next day, however, it was found out to be not Typhus but Smallpox. Then Monty put in a claim to nurse him, but you can imagine I was indignant and refused to budge. However, it was thought better that another should come to help, so Monty joined me. I can't describe those days; it was hardish work, as the servants caused us constant trouble. We did everything for him; no servant was allowed to come near his room. The Lord is able to make one equal to all occasions, and so we soon learnt the trade. Praise God, feelings were quite abolished, so that we were able to do what would ordinarily be the most revolting things with as little compunction as blowing one's nose."

"August [From Tai–Yuen he journeyed with Mr. Hudson Taylor to Hanchung.] As soon as we reached Hanchung, we heard of the Szchuan riots and that the foreigners had to flee for their lives from Chungking, whilst the houses had been destroyed. Mr. Taylor asked if there would be any volunteers to go into Szchuan, with the result, of course, that all volunteered. Thereupon it was arranged that I would go with Phelps and retake the place.

"Three days saw us at Pauling, where the inns would not take us in, as they had heard of the Chungking rows and wer e afraid of harbouring foreigners. So that night we slept in a room without a window, and one side of the room was next to the pigsty, the only partition being made of thin boards.

The next morning we were enabled to get into a small inn in another part of the city. This place had a window, to be sure, but the smells were even worse than before, whilst in the middle of the night I got up and commenced a pitched battle with some hundreds of—(rhymes with rugs), and bagged 25 brace to my own gun, without beaters or dogs, not bad for an hour's sport! On reaching Chungking, when the Consul saw us, it was as though he had seen a couple of ghosts. He said, 'However did you get here? There are guards on every gate in the city to prevent any "foreign devils" from coming in.' We said that God had brought us in and told him what we had come for. He said, 'No, you cannot stay here; I can give you a passport up or down the river, but no foreigners are allowed here except myself.' However, I stuck out against that, and after taking it quietly, he said, 'if you would like to stay in that hovel there, you can ; but there is no room for more than one.' Then we began to discuss which should stay. My friend was going to be married, and I was not, but he wanted to stay. Finally, the Consul asked us to dinner, and in the midst of dinner he turned to me and said, 'Studd, will you stay with me?' That settled the matter. I didn't know until some time afterwards why God had sent me to that place."

CHAPTER VII

HE GIVES AWAY A FORTUNE

BEFORE C.T. left England, he had a private interview with Mr. Hudson Taylor. By his father's will he was to inherit a large sum of money at the age of twentyfive, and the simple reading of the scriptures had led him to definite and far–reaching conclusions on the matter. The words of Christ, "Sell that ye have and give alms," and "Lay not up for yourselves treasures on earth"; the example of the early Church at Pentecost, of whom it says, "All that believed sold their possessions and goods and parted them to all men, as every man had need"; and finally the story of the rich young man to whom Jesus said, "One thing thou lackest: go thy way, sell that thou hast, and give to the poor, and thou shalt have treasure in heaven: and come take up thy cross and follow me," seemed to him to be as equally binding on himself as a present–day disciple of the Lord Jesus Christ, as on those to whom they were spoken. Therefore, in the light of God's Word he decided to give his entire fortune to Christ, and to take the golden opportunity offered him of doing what the rich young man had failed to do. It was no hasty decision, for Mr. Taylor pointed out that he did not actually inherit for two years and that, therefore, he could delay the final decision until then. But this was no question of feelings or emotion to C.T., or some special supernatural guidance which time might alter. It was simple obedience to the black and white statements of God's Word.

The two years passed and his 25th birthday found him alone at Chungking.

"One day [he writes] when I was reading the harmony of the Gospels, I came to where Christ talked with the rich young man. Then God seemed to bring back to me all the vows I had made. A few days later the post, which only came every half month, brought letters from the solicitor and banker to tell me what I had inherited. Then God made me just ordinarily honest and told me what to do. Then I learnt why I had been sent to Chungking. I needed to draw upon papers granting the power of attorney, and for that I had to have the signature of one of Her Majesty's officers. I went to the Consul, but when he saw the paper, he said, 'I won't sign it.' Finally, he said he would give me two weeks to think it over, and then if I still wished it, he would sign. At the end of two weeks I took it back and he signed it and off the stuff went. God has promised to give a hundredfold for everything we give to Him. A hundredfold is a wonderful percentage; it is 10,000 per cent."

So far as he could judge, his inherit ance was £29,000. But in order to leave a margin for error, he decided to start by giving £25,000. One memorable day, Jan. 13, 1887, he sent off four cheques of £5,000 each, and five of £1,000. As coolly and deliberately as a business man invests in some "gilt–edged" securities, as being both safe and yielding good interest, so C.T. invested in the Bank of Heaven. This was no fool's plunge on his part. It was his public testimony before God and man that he believed God's Word to be the surest thing on earth, and that the hundredfold interest which God has promised in this life, not to speak of the next, is an actual reality for those who believe it and act on it.

He sent £5,000 to Mr. Moody, expressing the hope that he would be able to start some Gospel work at Tirhoot in North India, where his father had made his fortune. Moody hoped to carry this out, but was unable to, and instead used the money to start the famous Moody Bible institute in Chicago, writing, "I will do the next best thing and open a Training School with it, from which men and women will go to all parts of the world to evangelize."

£5,000 he sent to Mr. George Müler £4,000 to be used on missionary work, and ?1,000 among the orphans; £5,000 to George Holland, in Whitechapel, "to be used for the Lord among His poor in London," asking for the receipt to be made out in his father's name, because of the spiritual help Mr. Holland had been to his father; and £5,000 to Commissioner Booth Tucker for the Salvation Army in India. This £5,000 arrived just after they had had a night of prayer for reinforcements vitally needed. It was used to send out a party of fifty new officers.

To Miss. McPherson for her work in London, to Miss Ellen Smyly in Dublin, General Booth of the Salvation Army, Rev. Archibald Brown in the East End of London, and Dr. Barnardo's Home, he sent £1,000 each.

In a few months he was able to discover the exact amount of his inheritance. He then gave some further thousands, mainly, to the C.I.M., leaving another £3,400 in his possession. The next chapters tell of his engagement and marriage. Just before the wedding he presented his bride with his money. She, not to be outdone, said, "Charlie, what did the Lord tell the rich young man to do?" "Sell all." "Well then, we will start clear with the Lord at our wedding." They then wrote the following letter to General Booth :

July 3, 1888.

"My dear General, We are so sorry last mail to hear of Mrs. Booth's serious illness, our hearts do go out in deep sympathy to you both. I cannot tell you how many times the Lord has blessed me through reading your and Mrs. Booth's addresses in *The War Cry* and your books. And now we want to enclose a cheque for £1,500. The other £500 has gone to Commissioner Tucker for his wedding present. Besides this I am instructing our Bankers, Messrs. Coutts and Co. to sell out our last earthly investment of £1,400 Consols and send what they realize to you. Henceforth our bank is in heaven. You see we are rather afraid–notwithstanding the great earthly safety of Messrs. Coutts and Co. and the Bank of England–we are, I say, rather afraid that they may both break on the Judgment Day. And this step has been taken not without most definite reference to God's Word, and the command of the Lord Jesus, who said, 'Sell that ye have and give alms. Make for yourselves purses which wax not old.' And He also said, 'If ye love Me, keep My commandments.' And again, 'He that said I know Him and keeps not His commandments is a LIAR.'

"We have felt the Spirit's drawings to this course after asking for a very long time, 'To whom shall we give it" Moreover, we have felt that in this way we shall better reach the people, as being the Lord Jesus' way of coming to preach Salvation. Hallelujah! We can also thank God by His grace that we have not done this by constraint, but cheerfully and of a ready mind and willing heart. Praise the Lord. Amen. "And we thank God too that now as regards England we are in that proud position, 'Silver and gold have I none.' But we don't want to be like Ananias and Sapphira, we tell you honestly we have a small amount out here, I myself at present don't know how much it is!

"Now this does not come from me, for I was told that the Bible says, 'He that provides not for his own house hath denied the faith and is worse than an infidel.' So I just took the whole pot and gave it to my little wife wherewith to provide for the household. And so now it is she who sends this money, regarding heaven as the safest Bank, and moreover thinking it is so handy; you have no trouble about cheques or rates of exchange, but just 'Ask and receive, that your joy may be full.'

"Now, good–bye, dear General, may the Lord keep you leading in this war for many years, and dear Mrs. Booth too. Our united heartfelt prayer is, God bless you both and all yours in both your inner and smaller and outer and larger families. Now there only remains one other command of the Lord Jesus for us to fulfil and that is, 'When thou doest thine alms, let not thy left hand know what thy right hand doeth, that thine alms may be in secret.' So therefore, in case that voracious friend of yours, *The War Cry*, should lay hold of this document and hold it up to the public gaze, we beg to sign ourselves–your loving, we know, and getting humble, we trust, would be Soldiers of Jesus Christ.

"MY WIFE AND ME."

"N.B.–Please also to enter the subscription as coming from 'Go and do thou likewise.' "

Readers will be able to watch for themselves the faithfulness of God to this young couple, how He fulfilled the promises, of which they had fulfilled the condition, during the forty–one years of their married life, not only to themselves, but to their children and the work of their hands; and may learn again the lesson from up–to–date evidences, "Blessed is the man that trusts in the Lord." Only eternity will reveal how many have been roused to face the real meaning of discipleship by the example of this twentieth–century "rich young man" who did leave all and follow Him.

CHAPTER VIII

AN IRISH GIRL AND A DREAM

PRISCILLA LIVINGSTONE STEWART arrived in Shanghai in 1887, one of a large party of new workers. She was Irish, from Lisburn, near Belfast; Irish in looks with blue eyes, lovely colour and golden hair, and Irish in spirit. She had only been converted eighteen months. A healthy, high–spirited girl, home life had given her the impression that religion was a longfaced affair, and thinking there was nothing in it for her, she had thrown herself into all the amusements of her set. But Christ captured her. And from the day that she saw the vision of the Man of Calvary and heard His voice saying, "With My stripes *you* are healed," she gave Him the full allegiance of her heart and stopped at nothing to witness for Him.

"I used to go to the meetings of the Salvation Army [she said]. I walked in their processions, and I tell you it was worthwhile in those days; there were old boots, wood, stones, rotten eggs and oranges thrown at us. None of my friends recognized me in the street, and all the young men who were fond of me walked on the other side."

She herself tells how it all came about :

"I am a Missionary now, but I was not made that way. Had you asked me to come to a meeting when I was a girl, I would have said, 'No, thank you, none of your religion for me'; for my idea of a person loving God was to have a face as long as a coffee pot, and I said, 'I have a young heart and a gay heart and I don't want to be made miserable, or to have a face as long as a fiddle!

"So right on till I was nearly out of my teens I maintained this attitude, not only of opposition when spoken to on such things, but also often scoffed and mocked and said, 'I will never serve God, I will never love Jesus nor call Him Lord and Master.' But what happened is just an illustration of 'Man proposes, but God disposes.'

"It was winter, and I had attended several small dances, and at last the day came, which is always a redletter day in every girl's life; I was to go to a ball! How little I thought it was to be my first and last ball! I thoroughly enjoyed it, dancing every dance, etc. It was a grand night! We got home at 4am. I went to bed and slept, but a disturbed sleep, as I had a horrible nightmare.

"The first time I awoke I tried to smother conscience with 'Oh, it's only a dream!' I slept again to awaken at the same point, but the third time conscience would not be silenced. So I got up, determined to drown all such nonsense in the reminiscences and laughter of the breakfast table with my cousins. But the pricks of conscience are not so easily smothered. For three months this nightmare worried me, for I became convinced that I had seen the end of my own existence.

"I had dreamed I was playing tennis, when suddenly I and those playing with me found ourselves surrounded by a multitude of people, and, as we stared in amazement, One rose high over all the crowd, and as He did so, I alone exclaimed, 'Why, that's the Son of God!' Looking and pointing straight at me, I distinctly heard Him say, 'Depart from me, for I never knew you.' The crowd seemed to disperse as clouds and we on that tennis court were left. I looked at my friends and seeing their expression of horror, turned to my special friend, saying, 'Never mind, we are all going together!'

"So hardened had I become that I did not care, though I knew and believed those words meant that I was cut off from God for ever. But as the days passed by, the thought fastened on my mind that somewhere in the Bible it said, 'It may be at evening, or at midnight, or at cockcrow that Jesus will come again,' and as each of these hours came round the thought arose, 'And if He comes, what about me?'

"At the end of three months I was staying with a lady who had herself been converted but recently. One night she was telling me some remarkable stories of tragedies and happenings in her family, and that her mother, who had been a wonderful woman, had often been prepared for coming troubles by visions or dreams sent her of God. I retorted, 'God has nothing to do with dreams. I can prove it. If I have been overstudying when I go to bed, my brain, being overwrought, goes on working, and I dream of my studies. If I eat things which disagree with me, they disturb my digestion, and when I sleep, I dream' ; and then I found myself trying to convince her of my theories by telling her that after the ball I suffered from a horrible nightmare, and in spite of myself I dared for the first time to tell another of the dream. Whilst doing so, I looked at her and suddenly came to my senses and wondered what I was doing in making such a confession, as she was looking at me in consternation. To turn off what I saw was coming, I laughed and said, 'Now God had nothing to do with that dream. That was the result of a supper of champagne and lobster and whirling round a ballroom all night.'

"But my friend exclaimed, 'Oh, child, if anyone has ever had a warning from God, you have; give Him your heart and nothing will ever disturb the peace of mind He will give you.' I was not conscious of wanting any such thing, but unlike my usual self, instead of mocking at such words, I found myself kneeling and saying, 'I have never decided for God, but I will to-night.' Then I realized I knew the devil as a person, as he actually seemed to come to my side, torturing me by bringing to remembrance all the times I had mocked and scoffed and said I would never love God nor yield my allegiance to Him. At the end of quite a time, a gentler influence seemed to overshadow me and a voice, oh, so different, asked, 'Child, what do you want?' 'To get to God, but I can't,' for there seemed veritably a great gulf fixed, and I, like Bunyan, with so great a load on me that I could not move. Suddenly close to me was raised the Cross with Jesus Christ nailed upon it, and with the crown of thorns upon His brow. Distinctly I saw the wounds and the riven side, and I saw the blood flow. Quickly the words came to me, just as to many a heathen woman I afterwards taught, 'Why wast Thou there?' And immediately a voice replied, 'With My stripes you are healed.' The vision of the Cross disappeared, my burden too, and I arose. My friend greeted me with, 'Well, what is it to be?' I said, 'I have seen Calvary, and henceforth He shall be my Lord and my God.'

"What I said would never be, God had brought to pass." Shortly after her conversion she gave herself to Christ for His service, and on opening the Bible for guidance one day, she saw on the margin of the Book these words in letters of light: "China, India, Africa,' These prophetic words were to be literally fulfilled."

Charlie Studd had never heard there was such a person as Priscilla Stewart when he arrived at Shanghai just about the same time. He had come to the coast for a different reason.

"In April I came down to the coast to Shanghai. My work in the West was done, and my road seemed to lie up to the North of China again. I heard that my brother G.B. would be out in Shanghai just about the time I would be arriving there. I got there about a fortnight before him. There was no chance of doing Chinese work in Shanghai for me, for the language was quite different from what we had up in the North and in the West, so I occupied my time with the sailors. Some ships of Her Majesty's Navy were in the Port, and there was a Sailors' Home, where we had nightly meetings which became hotter and hotter.

"On arriving in Shanghai I found one or two ladies, one the Superintendent of the Home, a Miss Black, a delightful soul. Then there was Mr. Stevenson, the Deputy Director, a real father to everybody, and lastly there was a young lady. I heard she was unable to go into the interior at present because she had heart trouble. After a few days Mr. Stevenson asked me my opinion about her. I replied I thought she had made a mistake in coming out, for she seemed as though the life had been eaten out of her, and she could never stand the interior. It seemed a real effort for her to get upstairs. Later on my opinion changed, as will be seen. One night she ventured to come to the soldiers' Meeting, again she came, and then she became a new creature, becoming the life and soul of that meeting. But there was something else that had influence upon her.

"A few months previous to my getting to Shanghai, I had received a letter from Booth Tucker of the Salvation Army, who was working in India. It was no ordinary letter. He described the life of the English lads and lasses he was leading in the evangelization of India. It stirred my soul.

My very dear Brother, [he wrote]

'I have been waiting to write to you, till I could give you some more definite news as to the special advances we hope to make by means of the help you have sent us. You will be glad to hear that the *first* result is a positive promise from the General to send us 50 firstclass officers as soon as possible. This is grand. For we feel that our special need is that of *sanctified flesh and blood* to carry on this war. After all the one great qualification now, as in the days of old, is the Baptism of the Holy Ghost. "Have you received the Holy Ghost since you believed?" ought to be asked of every wouldbe missionary. For lack of this how many failures are met with! No amount of education and talents can make up for so fatal a deficiency.

Here is an instance which has occurred since writing my first letter to you. We opened at Kandy, the capital of Ceylon, on Christmas eve. It has a population of about 30,000. We sent a simple Scotch lass and a rough native servant girl. The former is quite uneducated. Her orthography is–well, peculiar. She has been slow too at the language, and after three months' hard work could only speak a few sentences, giving her testimony, leading the meetings, etc. Her Lieut. knew no English. Yet the two went bravely in and took charge of a hall to hold about 250. They went in thoroughly as natives, had the hall packed from the first, got liberal collections in food and money, begged their midday meal. Result–in the course of about two months they had at least 100 souls and were able to enroll about fifty regular soldiers, several of whom have already been taken into the work as officers. Never before have native women been known to speak in public, but now there is a good band of them testifying nightly on the platform. Many of the converts are specially remarkable. One case was that of a deaf and dumb astrologer, who had to write out his experience and get it read!

'Our war is full of intense interest. We really never know what a day may bring forth. One hour we are fingering our food into our mouths (do you use chopsticks in China?), the next we are opening a letter from an anonymous friend with a donation of ?5,000! (We often tell the natives that if we were to get a lakh of rupees given to us, we should not buy an extra suit of clothes out of it. Most of us usually carry our wardrobes on our backs).

'You would, I am sure, delight in roughing it with us, or perhaps after your Chinese experiences it would appear smooth enough to you. Of one thing I feel sure, that having put your hand to the heathen plough, you will never, never look back, but will say, like some of our dear Indian (English) officers, "We would rather have the hardest station out here than the easiest in London."

···Our party have no salaries, get no money, and having food and raiment, they learn to be therewith content. No grumbling or arguing is heard in our camp. Both lads and lassies go bare foot (for preference). For meals they have rice water in the morning, rice and vegetable curries (no meat) at midday and the same in the evening. The use of tea and coffee is quite given up as being too European! The floor of the quarters being well raised and dug, we have abolished beds. There are no chairs and tables in the camp. I am myself sitting squatted on a mat, with my papers round me on the floor. Nevertheless, we really are very comfortable and as happy as possible. Most beautiful of all has been the spirit of unity, love, devotion and sacrifice which has animated them all from the first. We have constant victory and God is showing us how to manage and train these officers and manufacture them into real natives··· Remember that mere soul–saving is comparatively easy work and is not nearly so important as that of manufacturing the saved ones into *Saints, Soldiers and Saviours*.

'We are praying and believing for you. The Lord of the Harvest abundantly bless you, enable you to see and fall in line with His notions for a present day salvation sweep. Oh, that we may see eye to eye with the Lord in His plans for saving men! I often think what fools we shall reckon ourselves to have been when we get to heaven and see what we might have been and done with the aid of a little more salvation gumption!'

"One day at morning prayers I asked Mr. Stevenson if I might read the letter to those who were worshipping with us. There was not a soul in all that company that was not stirred by that letter–stirred to the depths. It told of the joy with which others were facing a very hard life in order to save the souls of the Indians. It created a sort of competition: why not try and go one better?

"No doubt that letter stirred Miss. Steward. She became a nightly attendant at the Soldiers' Rest. These meeting abide in my memory chiefly through two persons. One was a Quartermaster–Sergeant, if there is such a person in the Navy; anyhow, he was the leader of all the men from the "Sapphire," which was the name of the boat. The other was Miss Stewart. Her messages were all fire–the fire that burns into people's souls. I think I led the meetings, and these two did the work. On one occasion an officer came; he got converted. Pretty well nightly there were souls converted, till there became quite a band of them. These would return to their ship, but not to their bunks. They loitered about the deck to look after any late arrivals who had imbibed a spirit other than their own; they would take charge of these, would get them to a quieter part of the deck, and one or two would hold them up while the others got down on their knees and prayed. Many of them they prayed sober, and got down to their bunks without any official observation. Not a few became converted and would be introduced to me the next night at the meeting as trophies.

"There was no convention about our meetings. There is one incident that was quite peculiar. We had a testimony, and we wanted to sing off our joy, so I gave out 'Stand up for Jesus'; but for some reason or other, I cannot remember why, we were already standing, so I said, 'Here, this isn't enough, we are already standing; we must do something else for Jesus.' So I shouted, 'Stand on your chairs for Jesus!' Any man who knows Jack knows with what alacrity they would jump on to their chairs! And how they grinned from ear to ear! 'Stand up for Jesus' had never been sung so vociferously before. Of course, Miss Stewart was on her chair too. There was but one man who would not take the chair, and I am ashamed to say that man was a missionary. That missionary escorted Miss Stewart home, and expressed himself pretty strongly

"What things were gain to me, those I counted loss for Christ"

THE THREE CRICKETING BROTHERS
J.E.K. C.T. G.B.
Captains of Cambridge University, 1882-3-4

THE CAMBRIDGE SEVEN
C.T. Studd, M. Beauchamp, S.P. Smith
A.T. PolhillTurner, D.E. Hoste, C.H. PolhillTurner, W.W. Cassels

PRISCILLA STEWART
AT THE TIME OF THE BALL (see p.71)

MRS. C. T. STUDD IN 1921
"THE MOTHER OF W.E.C. AND H.A.M."

about the breach of good manners it was to get anybody to stand on chairs at a religious meeting. The end of the story comes a little later.

"Meanwhile my brother came. He was travelling for his health to avoid the severity of an English winter. He had been converted some ten years before, but had grown cold. He slept in my room at the Mission. I made a point of not speaking to him about religious things. The day after his arrival he booked his passage to Japan by a boat leaving a week afterwards, but he never sailed by it. The first few days he was much up at the Club playing cricket on their ground, and made a large score which advertised things a bit, for, of course, I went to see him, play, and of course, people wanted to know how this brother of his had 'gone mad.' My brother showed them very efficiently by 'going mad' himself before the whole of Shanghai, and getting up in a public meeting and telling them all about it. The consequence was that my brother, instead of going to Japan, came into the interior of China with me. 'If you, Charlie,' he afterwards said to me, 'had tackled me on religion when we were rooming together, I should have sailed in that boat to Japan.' The leadings of God are often mysterious but always perfect.

"My impression of Shanghai in those day was a remarkable one. The Spirit of God seemed to have come down upon the place. You could go out at midnight on the streets and find even the police anxious to talk about their souls. Miss Stewart was getting visibly better. She would run up the stairs three at a time. She began to sing all sorts of songs she had picked up at the Salvation Army before coming out to China–songs set to secular tunes. It did not matter to us what other people thought, we praised the Lord with a loud voice, our hearts being filled with joy, for manifestly the Lord was working with us."

G.B.'s letters to his mother told the same story; "May 27. You will see by my writing thus that a change has come over me, and I know now it is just in answer to prayer; for Charlie had got Mr. Stevenson, Mr. McCarthy and others to pray for me before I came, that I might receive just this distinct blessing, that I might surrender willingly to the Lord Jesus Christ. And oh, I have felt the Spirit striving within me, and I felt such a hungry, unsatisfied craving that I can't tell you what peace and joy the Lord has given me in believing." "June 3. There is a Miss Stewart here who has lately co me out to the Mission, and has been wonderfully used of God. Doors have been opening to her right and left, and in several houses she has been the means of bringing people on to their knees in drawing–rooms where I do not suppose anyone ever knelt to the Lord before. I have never been so happy in my life. I can't cease praising the Lord that he has given me grace to come out boldly for Him and to surrender myself wholly for His service. Truly the Christian life is a happy one when it is all for Jesus."

"June 9. The men on the "Sapphire" are holding the fort grandly, and numbers have been added to the Church on board. Charlie has been most indefatigable, and these fellows love him as much as he loves them."

And when leaving China, G.B. wrote to C.T. :

"Dec. 6. Oh, Charlie, I have been praising the Lord for the wisdom He gave you in dealing with me at Shanghai, the love with which you spoke to me and didn't urge me with importunity. I do see so clearly the Lord's hand guiding you in it."

"But all good things must end [continued C.T.]. My brother and I must go up North, and Miss Stewart into the centre of China. She went first. She was travelling alone by steamer on the Yangtse river. She left at night. In the morning she found one of her fellow–passengers was the missionary who refused to stand on the chair for Jesus. They got into conversation and she found that he was troubled in his soul. He said, 'I believe in the Saviour, and I suppose that I am going to heaven, but I see that you people have got quite a different religion from mine. I have not got this abounding joy that seems to take utter possession of you.' Miss. Stewart began to poke about to see where the lack was, and naturally she said, 'Are you willing to do anything for Jesus? If you are willing to do anything for Jesus the same as we are, God is no respecter of persons, and will surely give you the same joy as we have.' 'Well,' he said, 'I don't know that there is anything I would not do for Jesus. I admit that I refused to stand on the Chair for Jesus, and I don't seem to have had much peace since that incident.'

'Well,' said Miss. Stewart, 'I think I should get rid of that if I were you.' But he said, 'What can I do? There is no meeting here.' 'Well,' said Miss Stewart, 'if I were you I should stand on my chair for Jesus.' 'What!' he said, 'here on the ship?' 'Yes,' she said, 'right here on the ship.' This young doctor was lost in thought, but he meant business, for presently he got up and went into the saloon and stood on the chair for Jesus. Whether he sang or merely read the hymn I don't know, but I know he returned from the saloon a different man from the one who entered it."

CHAPTER IX

UNITED TO FIGHT FOR JESUS

PRISCILLA Stewart went to work with three other ladies in the inland city of Ta–Ku–Tang. C.T. returned to Taiyuen–Fu, in the far North. A lively correspondence went on between them which could only have one end, but Miss Stewart was not too easily persuaded, for the first letter dates from June 9, but the engagement was not till October 5! There was always a controversy as to how it came about. C.T.'s version is this :

"I think there is always a little difficulty as to how it came about. She said I wrote to her; I say she spoke to me, I do not say with her eyes, not with her tongue–she was keeping that in reserve– she spoke with her acts. I did not marry her for her pretty face; I married her for her handsome actions towards the Lord Jesus Christ and those He sent her to save. In fact, I can well remember the afternoon when I was sitting, talking to a missionary in Taiyuen and he twitted me on being engaged to the prettiest girl in all Shanghai. Now that, I tell you in all truth, was an absolute shock to me, for certainly I had never thought of her pretty face. In fact, till this day I verily believe that of all God's many good gifts, the least of all is good looks."

Miss. Stewart's version is this :

"If C.T. were here, he would tell you I had proposed to him. I did not: as a matter of fact, for certain reasons I refused him. And when I tell you his answer, you will see it is just characteristic of the man. His reply was, 'You have neither the mind of God nor the will of God in the matter, but I have. And I intend to marry you whether you will or not, so you had better make up your mind and accept the situation.' What was I to do? That is the reason why I am Mrs. C.T. today."

But documentary evidence gives the verdict to Miss Stewart, for she kept his love–letters, and in one of them we find this :

"July 25, 1887. But here I do say that after 8 days spent alone in prayer and fasting, I do believe the Lord has shown me that your determination is wrong and will not stand, and that you yourself will see this presently, if the Lord has not shown you already...

"Day after day passes and I only get more and more convinced about it, and I cannot doubt it is of the Lord, for you know somewhat of how I have spent the time since receiving your letter : everything else has been laid aside, occupation, sleep and food, and I have sought His face and to know His will, and He has led me straight forward, and day by day He speaks to me and gives me encouragement and emboldens me to ask definitely for you."

Remarkable love–letters they are too, full of the consuming passion of his life, fuller by a long way of message from the Bible, and plans for spending their lives for Christ, than of her. She, being a sensible woman, bound him over to burn hers, so only one has survived. Two of his, written when he was recovering from a serious illness, run into 68 and 69 pages respectively of tiny writing! The following are one or two extracts :

"July 25. It will be no easy life, no life of ease which I could offer you, but one of toil and hardship; in fact, if I did not know you to be a woman of God, I would not dream of asking you. It is to be a fellow soldier in His Army. It is to live a life of faith in God, a fighting life, remembering that here we have no abiding city, no certain dwelling place, but only a home eternal in the Father's House above. Such would be the life: may the Lord alone guide you."

"Oct. 8. Now before I go further, I just want to beseech you, darling, that we may both make the same request every day to our Father, that we may give each other up to Jesus every single day of our lives to be separated or not just as He pleases, that neither of us may ever make an idol of the other.

"I must write and tell darling mother this mail, and others too, for I cannot keep it secret; only I do laugh when I think of how little I know of or about you, my own darling, not even your age or anything; only it is more than enough for me that you are a true child and lover of the Lord Jesus, that He has knit my heart to yours and yours to mine to work together for Him with all our hearts and souls and minds till He come."

"Oct. 14. I remember at Pingyang two years ago four or five of us young bachelors were talking about marriage, and most of us (and I among them) were rather against it and for using the utmost caution–please don't laugh, don't roar–and then at last I said, 'Well, please God I don't want to marry, but if I do, I want to marry a real Salvation Army Hallelujah Lassie,' which was received with much laughter. Well, here the Good Lord has just taken me at my word.

"Now that about the wedding garments brings me to a very practical question, viz. : No smart wedding clothes for us–just our ordinary clothes, as plain as can be, and I am for being registered at the Consul's and then having a real Hallelujah meeting, just something all for Jesus. We are strangers and pilgrims here, and I vote we have a real pilgrim's wedding.

"I love you for your love to Jesus, I love you for your zeal towards Him, I love you for your faith in Him, I love you for your love for souls, I love you for loving me, I love you for your own self, I love you for ever and ever. I love you because Jesus has used you to bless me and fire my soul. I love you because you will always be a red hot poker making me run faster. Lord Jesus, how can I ever thank Thee enough for such a gift?"

"Nov. 10. Oh Scilla, in China it is a life and death struggle. If *we* don't really die daily, our souls will, and we shall have to be shelved. Let us rather go home broken down in health than broken down spiritually. Yes, by God's grace we will live Captain Soul and Lieutenant Body, and if need be we will die Captain Soul and Lieutenant Body. Scilla darling, let us be in travail for these Chinese. Oh, Holy Ghost, leave us not alone, stir us up and that continually. Quicken us, O Lord, and make us to run in the way of Thy commandments.

"I stick to the Chinese food by myself, and the Lord has just given me a huge big blessing through taking the stand. You can little imagine how the devil tried ever so hard to get me to cave in and go the easy path. It was a cross having to go and tell the

T–s that I was not going to feed with them. I feel more than ever that I have done the right thing. I went to lunch with them, and everything there just confirmed me in living Chinese and in wanting to get lower and lower; and I could not help thinking, Why, these poor Chinese must think we foreigners think a lot of our stomachs. I feel it must be a bit awkward for the T–s, for the different styles must bring thoughts up to them, with their table–cloths, napkins, foreign ware and food, whilst I have naught but my bowl and chopsticks. No table–cloths and napkins for us, old girlie!"

"Jan. 10. My prescription for you is to sing daily :

"Jesus I love thee,
Thou art to me
Dearer than ever
Charlie can be!"

His description of her to his mother was very illuminating:

"I suppose you want to know about her. Well, to tell you the truth, I can't tell you much except about her spiritual life and her life before the world; I don't even know her age, but guess she is some years my junior, don't know though. She ain't very big, and as regards her face, well, she has the beauty of the Lord her God upon her, which is worth more than all the beauty of the whole world. She writes a very good letter, all about Jesus, and naturally a big hand except when she has a lot to say; and she can run up and down stairs a tremendous pace ; she can also play the harmonium or organ and sing a bit, but her voice wasn't wonderful in Shanghai. She's very fond of the Salvation Army hymns (so am I), and of the

Salvation Army too (so am I), and she doesn't fear the face of man or woman a little bit, I do believe ; but just fires away at everybody she meets about their souls. I haven't got a photo of her at all, so I cannot give you even a guess at what she is like, probably Georgie is a better hand at such descriptions and will be able to satisfy your curiosity.

"Oh! I know one thing more ; her name is Priscilla Livingstone Stewart, and she calls herself 'Scilla' (rum name, ain't it?) Why not 'Pris.,' I don't understand, but then she's 'Oirish.' "

The official wedding was at the coast, whither they had to travel to find an English Consul to perform the ceremony. They had an unofficial wedding first, performed by the well–known Chinese Evangelist, Pastor Shi, at Miss. Stewart's Station.

Pastor Shi had been paying a visit to the four ladies. They had unburdened their hearts to him about their great longing to reach the people of the city, and the barriers in the way owing to their sex. They had already been trying several schemes, although at risk of their reputations. The ordinary Chinese women wore trousers, and only the upper class mandarin's wife a skirt, so they took to trousers in order to be on a level with the "common people." For this reason men missionaries were forbidden to visit their Station. Then Miss Stewart used to take a Chinese teacher and go out to buy silk at a shop, always walking in the proper fashion, some yards behind the teacher. She used to remain haggling in the shop as long as she could, well knowing a large crowd would gather, while the teacher talked to the crowd.

But when Pastor Shi arrived, they asked him to institute an open–air meeting outside their own door.

He agreed, and the first open–air meeting was held in that city.

"He preached, and we four girls got on our knees. It was March, and was sleeting and snowing. The street was running with water and melted snow; we had on our padded cotton trousers, and prayed while Pastor Shi preached the Gospel. Having given us the courage to do so ourselves, when he went away, two of our number carried on with the singing, for they had lovely voices and played the guitar. We two did not yet know the language. I never saw tears in a Chinaman's eyes except in those days when we girls knelt and prayed for their souls; but on those occasions I saw the tears coursing down their cheeks, and I had heard nobody report such a thing before."

But the result to Miss Stewart of kneeling in the snow was an attack of pneumonia. She was so seriously ill that the other workers decided to send for her fianc?. He himself had been at death's door for weeks with pleurisy in both lungs, typhoid, and then pneumonia, being devotedly nursed back to life by his brother G.B. But he had recovered just in time to respond to the call and go to Miss Stewart. She turned the corner, and when she began to get better, the Chinese said that as her fianc? had come all that way to see her, they must be married at once. Mr. Studd agreed with them! So they had a sham marriage. Pastor Shi was not a licensed man, but they let him "marry" them in order to please the Chinese and settle their minds. Pastor Shi insisted on Mr. Studd being rigged out in a new hat and a pair of shoes which the Pastor produced. The shoes got so uncomfortable that during the wedding he had to slip out of them. He was also exceedingly tired after the strain of nursing his bride, and so fell asleep during his own wedding address. The bride wore a long white sash and on it these words, "United to fight for Jesus." At the end of the ceremony they both knelt and made a solemn promise to God, “We will never hinder one another from serving Thee.” Then they travelled down to Tientsin, where they were married by the Consul.

“Tientsin. Scilla is now staying with a Dr. and Mrs. Irwin, they are so kind. I am in a Chinese inn by myself at any rate until Saturday, when we go to the Consul.

We are going to be married in our ordinary clothes, just common native calico ones: the people cannot quite understand and were horrified when it first came out that we had not got any wedding garments and didn’t intend to get any.”

CHAPTER X

PERILS AND HARDSHIPS IN INLAND CHINA

THE young couple went straight from their wedding ceremony to open work in an inland city, Lungang–Fu. They were accompanied by Miss Burroughes, Mrs. Studd's friend and fellow–worker, and later by Miss Edith Bewes. It was a very different China from that of today, danger, insult and in many cases martyrdom, was the price paid for bringing the Saviour to them.

"The first house we had was a haunted house. It was the only one we could get in that city. We were determined to go where there was no European. Of course there were no houses to be had by the foreign devils, but a wicked old man owned this house, and he let us have it, as it was haunted. It was just bare white washed walls, and brick floors, but very unevenly bricked, with a fire–

place in the centre, and a brick bed. Our mattress was a cotton wool quilt about an inch thick. That was our bed for the first three years, until it became so infested with scorpions that we had to have it pulled down. Then we had a wooden sort of planking.

"For five years we never went outside our doors without a volley of curses from our neighbours. Gradually we got on familiar terms with the people, by allowing them to inspect our apartments, examine everything and pry into all our belongings at their own sweet will. Then when the curiosity of three months was sated, our method of reviving interest was a mixture of rit ualistic practices wit h those of the Salvation Army–a banjo and a procession were combined.

"Everything that happened in that city the Chinese blamed on us. There was a year of drought. Our lives were at stake, for they held us responsible. They made a five days' journey to send for a certain god : he was to be brought and was to have the sun down on his own pate. On a certain day they put up placards saying that everybody in the city was to have their big doors shut in their courtyards, and outside there was to be incense burning to this god. They knew we would not place incense outside our door, and they meant to riot our house. I was very ill at the time. Mr. Studd feared it was going to be pretty bad. They began to throw glass and brick–bats at us, and then to pull down the chapel. Mr. Studd had turned all the Chinese Christians out of the compound and told them to go home. He carried me right into the court; then he climbed the wall and went to see the mandarins. He found that they were out of the city. They knew it was no good supporting the foreign devils, as their people would turn on them. This was how we escaped. Among the crowd there was a man of letters, as they call him out here–a teacher. He said to the crowd, 'What are you doing? Whilst you are wasting the time, the day is passing, and if you do not take the god on quickly, he will not feel the sun on his own pate. Take him on, and then come back this way.' They think a lot of a man of letters, and so they meekly turned and took up the stone god. They never came back, but returned by another route where the rich people live, looted their houses, and stole the silver they had promised to give to the city from which they had got the god."

In this apparently barren soil, they had wonderful evidences of the power of the Gospel both in melting hard heart and in producing men of God whom no persecution could move.

"On one occasion [writes C.T.] my wife was speaking to a Chinese woman who had called, telling her of the Gospel. The woman seemed interested, so she showed her a picture of the crucifixion. As the woman heard the story of the sacrifice on Calvary, she burst into tears.

"Another occasion was the first time we ever showed a magic lantern. Never shall I forget the effect of the crucifixion scene, nor the prayer of the chief of our Christians. He was a good man, but as is so often the case, his attitude was that there was not much value in self–sacrifice, but that the display of money, and holding out advantages to the people would bring the crowds, and with the crowds the blessing. But the crucifixion scene broke him all up. His prayer was one long sob, and he was never the same man again."

There was a man who refused to be styled a Christian until he had "acted it out"; there was another who had been on his own confession the biggest blackguard in the province.

"At the end of an address on the text, 'He is able to save to the uttermost ' [said C.T.], after t he congregation had left, a single

Chinaman remained behind, right at the back of the room. When we went to him, he told us we had been talking sheer nonsense. He said, 'I am a murderer, an adulterer, I have broken all the laws of God and man again and again. I am also a confirmed opium smoker. He cannot save me.' We laid before him the wonders of Jesus and His gospel and His power. The man meant business, and was soundly converted. He said, 'I must go to the town where I have done all this evil and sin, and in that very place tell the good tidings.' He did. He gathered crowds, was brought before the mandarin, and was ordered 2,000 strokes with the bamboo, till his back was one mass of red jelly, and he himself was thought to be dead. He was brought back by some friends, taken to the hospital and nursed by Christian hands, till he was, at last, able to sit up. He then said, 'I must go back again to–,' his own city, 'and preach this Gospel.' We strongly dissuaded him, but a short time after he escaped and started preaching in the same place. Once more he was brought before the court. They were ashamed to give him the bamboo again, so sent him to prison. But the prison had small open windows and holes in the wall. Crowds collected, and he preached out of the windows and holes; till, finding he did more preaching inside the prison than out, they set him free, in despair of ever being able to move one so stubborn and so staunch. Such men are worth saving."

There was Mr. Fan, the most reliable evangelist on the Station, of whom C.T. tells the following story: "One of our servants, as he came back from the market, came to my wife and myself and said, 'Oh, you should just see Mr. Fan walking up the street. He walks as no other man walks.' 'No, I suppose he goes on all fours.' But the boy was not to be put off. 'Oh, no,' he said, 'everybody else who walks up the street is always looking this way and that way to see everything that can be seen, and nodding to this one and that one, but our Mr. Fan, he sets his nose right in front of him and marches after it; he neither looks to the right nor to the left, and he does not care who is there or anywhere; he only thinks of one thing, and that is the object of his walking up the street.' There is a great deal more in that description than meets the eye."

A great deal of Mr. Studd's time was occupied by the Opium Refuge which he opened for the wretched victims of the drug. As many as fifty would be there at a time. "We started to take in and cure Opium Sots. Two came. A month saw them cured, a wonder unto many and unto themselves. Then they came in crowds." During the seven years about 800 of these men and women passed through the Refuge, and some went away saved as well as cured.

Four little people came to brighten their Chinese home; a fifth was with them only for one day. They never had a doctor on any of these occasions, choosing rather to go on with their work and trust the Lord than go the necessary long journey and be away for so long a time. It was a direct touch of the Lord which saved Mrs. Studd at the birth of their first child in 1889.

"There was no doctor then within days [writes C.T.], neither a nurse. The question came, should we leave our work three months before the time in order to have the skill of the doctor at our disposal and then wait another two months until Scilla was strong enough to travel–five months away from our work? It could not be done! Why not have Dr. Jesus? And so she settled it.

"The time came. Scilla had had two months' training in Queen Charlotte's Hospital in London. She found her self having t o act no t only t he par t o f t he wouldbe mother, but also that of her own doctor.

But we had an assistant. Being a male he was as useless as I was, as the world would say, but I am not sure that he was not the most efficient of the three of us, for his father was a doctor, and he knew the seriousness of the case. He was in the adjoining room never ceasing to pray for us. This assistant was Stanley Smith. I am sure I need not assure you that Dr. Jesus managed things perfectly. It was not till some days afterwards that a lady missionary turned up who was skilled in such matters as these. Of course, she at once relieved me of the greater part of the nursing, but alas, to our consternation, there was a relapse.

"Something went wrong [he wrote to his mother], and poor Scilla suffered fearfully. Miss Kerr tried all she knew, but it was no use; poor Scilla got weaker and weaker, and it seemed she must die. Miss Kerr said to me, 'She is just breaking up altogether and can never live in China. You had better take her home, if she can come through this.' This seemed to rouse me from sleep, a sleep of sorrow and anxiety and fatigue, and I said, 'We will give our lives out here willingly, but we will not go home unless the Lord distinctly sends us home.' I felt the Lord must hear and heal, for we had trusted Him and He is so faithful; so I said, 'Well, let us anoint Scilla and ask God to raise her up.' Miss Kerr did not see her way clearly to do that; so as Miss Burroughes was ill also, it devolved on me only. Scilla was of the same mind, so I knelt down and in the name of the Lord anointed her with oil. Immediately the trouble ceased. So remarkable was it that in the morning, when Miss Kerr came to nurse her, she said, 'What has happened? Why, you are well.' Scilla told her I had anointed her and prayed, and she said, 'Well, it is marvellous.' So, although we are poor sinners and nothing at all, the Lord nevertheless hears us when we cry."

"I had five children[1] [Mrs. Studd wrote in later years] and I never saw a doctor. God did wonderfully. One of the curses of China is not to let their little girls live. They say they have the trouble of bringing them up, and then when they are married, the dowry they receive does not make up for all that has been spent on them. I went into a mother's house once and found her groaning, and asked where the baby was. It was born at daylight and immediately it was just thrown into the moat or into the pagodas which are built for this purpose with a certain hole, so that the wolves can jump in and get the baby when they want it. How many times have I come home brokenhearted. God gave me four little girls.

He gave me them for a purpose. He wanted these people to learn a lesson. We called our first girl Grace, we called the other Praise (Dorothy), Prayer (Edith), and the last one, Joy (Pauline). They thought Mr. Studd must be a strange man to call the fourth Joy. We wanted them to learn that God loves little girls as well as little boys.

"We lost one child and on that occasion, I was absolutely alone with Mr. Studd. Mr. Stanley Smith came over when he heard I was desperately ill. He arrived just in time to help Mr. Studd who had gone to the city and bought a little pigskin box to put the little figure in, and to bury it. I was left alone in my room. I shall never forget that experience. It has stuck to me through life. I felt absolutely broken hearted, and the quest ion was whet her I was going to give in and t he who le of missionar y life be wrecked.

1 A sixth was born after their return to England, a boy, but he only lived two days.

Therefore, whilst Mr. Studd was with Mr. Smith, I made a mark in my Bible. I made a covenant with my God that I was not going to let sorrow of any kind come into my life and ruin my life as a missionary. I was not going to let my husband see sorrow that would unhinge him. He never saw a tear when he came back." We are not told by what means the Lord regularly supplied their financial needs these years, for when they left Tientsin on their wedding day, their worldly possessions were "five dollars and some bedding." But God gave them one signal opportunity of proving that it is as easy for Him to supply the needs of His servants in the heart of China as in the middle of London, although not a human soul may know about it.

"My own family knew nothing of our circumstances [wrote C.T.], only that we were in the heart of China. The last of our supplies was finished, and there was no apparent hope of supplies of any kind coming from any human source. The mail came once a fortnight. The mail man had just set out that afternoon, and in a fortnight he would bring the return mail. The children were put to bed. Then my wife came to my room. We had looked facts in the face. If the return of the postman brought no relief, starvation stared us in the face. We decided to have a night of prayer. We got on our knees for that purpose. I think we must have stayed there twenty minutes before we rose again. We had told God everything that we had to say in those twenty minutes. Our hearts were relieved; it did not seem to us either reverence or common sense to keep on talking to God as though He were deaf or could not understand our simple language, or the extremity of our circumstances, or the weight of the words of His Son, who said that God knew everything before we told Him, or as He said himself,

'Before they call I will answer." And verily He did. The mail man returned at the appointed time. We were not slow to open the bag. We glanced over the letter; there was nothing, and we looked at each other. I went to the bag again, took it by the corners and shook it mouth downwards; out came another letter, but the handwriting was totally unfamiliar to us. Drawn blank again. I opened it and then began to read. We were different after the reading of that letter from what we had been before, and I think our whole lives have been different since. This was the letter–I looked at the signature first, one wholly unknown to me–'I have,' he said, 'for some reason or other received the command of God to send you a cheque for £100. I have never met you, I have only heard of you, and that not often but God has prevented me from sleeping tonight by this command. Why He should command me to send you this I don't know–you will know better than I. Anyhow, here it is and I hope it will do you good.' The name of that man was Frank Crossley. We had neither of us seen each other or corresponded."

CHAPTER XI

ON THE AMERICAN CAMPUS

THEY returned home in 1894, after ten years in China. The year previously C. T. had almost died. In a few rough sheets Mrs. C. T. had scribbled the following (for neither kept a regular diary) :

"March 27, 1893. Charlie very ill all day seemed as if the Lord about to take him. We did all we could to relieve him, but in vain. About 4.30 p.m. he asked to be anointed. We anointed him, Fan, Liu, Reni, Guer, Jangso, Mrs. Wang, Mrs. Jang and Mrs. Liu all present. About 12 p.m. breathing lighter and better. Morning much better.

"April 2. Tried to find out Charlie's heart's thoughts about going home or leaving China. He said the Lord had not told him to go home. It was a solemn thing to leave the station where God had placed you, unless you had a direct message from God to do so, and he had not received that message. He could trust God and no one else."

The guidance must have come next year, although we are not told how. The journey had to be made, right through China with four small children, Pauline, the youngest, still a baby in arms.

"It was a long cavalcade that travelled the five miles to the first village of our journey. It was not our cavalcade that was long, but the people who came to escort us. Everyone had to turn back at the village to get into the city before the gates were closed at dark. Just as I entered the village, the two Chinese nurses of our children came up with the tears streaming down their faces, and said to me, 'Oh, Pastor, you will take care of the children, won't you?' And in among their sobs there was no other leavetaking but just that, 'Oh, Pastor, you will take care of our children now we are gone.' Humour is a great thing in the Mission Field, and a touch of it will win the day when the heart is sad to a degree.

"We dared not take women on a journey to the coast to nurse our children because of the effect of hostile reports to the tune that we were going to steal these two women and take them to the land of the foreign devils. So we had two young men as nurses, and they were every bit as devoted and as efficient as the two middle–aged women. Never shall I forget the scene at Shanghai, when at last it dawned upon these two that the final separation had come. There in front of the whole ship's company were these two grown–up Chinese men sobbing their hearts out, and their sobbing was by no means soundless. I was waving a last good–bye when a fellow–passenger touched my arm and said, 'Well, Mr. Studd, you didn't come out to China for nothing.'

"The going home was no easy job with four young children. Part of the journey was by sedan chairs carried by mules, another part by cargo boat on the river, where sleeping was accomplished on the top of boxes of uneven height. It was the time of the war between Japan and China. The Chinese had no idea of the various countries which composed the world; their idea was that there was one vast middle kingdom as they call it, represented by a huge circle. That was China, of course. The circle was fitted in a square, and the four empty spaces at the corners of the square where the circle did not touch, and which embraced all the rest of the world, was occupied by one kingdom, which they called 'The Kingdom of the Foreign Devils.' Consequently they thought that we English and the Japanese were one, and the people spread it about that my father was one of those who had rebelled against China. When we got on the river nearer to Tientsin, things were sometimes pretty ugly, and wherever our boat(now a house–boat) touched the banks, a vast crowd assembled to see the foreign devils. But, as usual, God arranged for our deliverance in a strange way. The eldest of our four girls spoke Chinese, and the crowd caught sight of her and asked her a question, 'What is your age, and your name, and have you any food?' and so on. To their amazement she answered back in Chinese. The result was an ugly crowd became an admiring one, and they would arrange for relays of Chinese to come up and ask the same questions. The Chinese on every occasion summed up the matter with the same sentences: 'You see, this child talks our language because she eats our food.'

" At Shanghai we got on to a German Lloyd steamer. Of course, we travelled second class, but the stewards were all musicians and made quite a band, which performed every afternoon in our saloon. We appreciated that band more than most people ever knew, for our four children took seats to listen, so we could get a little rest.

About the third day we heard the pitterpatter of feet coming to the cabin, and the three elder ones burst in in a state of considerable excitement, saying, 'We do not understand these missionaries at all, for they only play music, and they never sing hymns nor pray.' In their life in the interior of China they had never seen any white man or woman who was not a missionary!

"We arrived home in London eventually, and were most royally entertained by my mother at her home in Hyde Park Gardens. The children did not know any English. My mother had most generously provided a nurse to look after them, so that we might have an easier time and see more of our friends. The nurse found she had bitten off a little more than she could chew on some occasions, especially when once she punished one of the four by locking her up in the bathroom. This was too much for 'The Clan,' who got round her and would not leave go of her skirts nor stop talking vociferous Chinese, until the door was unlocked and the other member of the Clan rejoined them.

"On one occasion a cousin of mine and her husband were staying with my mother. He took a delight in playing with my girls, but being a business man he had to escape, and this was not always an easy thing. One day he had just escaped. Our girls knowing only Chinese, were unacquainted with the pronouns of the masculine and feminine gender–they had all plumped for 'She' and called everybody 'Lady'–so they rushed up to us in great trouble and said, 'Where has that lady gone?' (they had just begun to learn a little English by this time).

"Not knowing what had happened, we said, 'What lady?' 'Oh,' they said, 'that lady that always plays with us.' Now we knew that the lady of the two was quite a proper person, and so we said, 'But what lady?' Their reply was, 'Oh, you know quit e well; it is the lady wit h no hair on the top of her head.' I was afterwards told that gentleman was for some considerable time known by not a few of his associates in the city by that description."

A spell at home was now a necessity. Both C. T. and his wife were very poorly. It was even feared lest his lungs were affected, though it only turned out to be due to severe overstrain and poor nourishment. But furlough to C. T. was only a change of battle fronts. If God ordered him home, very well, he would go out for souls at home just as he had gone out for them in China. Health should be no deterrent. Star Hall, Manchester, where he and Frank Crossley became very close friends, the Universities, and many other places were visited. On one occasion he was invited to North Wales. He had always prayed and looked out for opportunities of winning members of his own family to Christ. Now he was to have a chance. Dr. Edwardes, the Principal of a Theological College, had asked him to come and talk to the students, and be his guest. This news reached the ears of his cousin, Mrs. George Thomas, who was living near by. She at once wrote to Dr. Edwardes and said that they could not think of allowing Charlie to come up there without staying with them, and so would he mind letting him come to them. He struck a very wise bargain and replied that he would, on condition that Mrs. Thomas attended the meetings. Mrs. Thomas agreed, so when C. T. arrived, she accompanied him to the afternoon meeting. In the course of his talk he said, "True religion is like the smallpox. If you get it, you give it to others and it spreads." This was too much for Mrs. Thomas, and on the way home she said indignantly, "What an awful thing you said this afternoon, Charlie, comparing religion to smallpox. I thought it disgusting!" This led to a long talk. According to her promise, she went with him again to the evening meeting. She was obviously hit and very silent on the way home. She made him a cup of cocoa and handed it to him as he sat on the sofa in the drawing room. But he went on talking, while she stood there holding out the cup. She spoke to him, but he still ignored it. Then she naturally got annoyed. "Well," he said, "that is exactly how you are treating God, Who is holding out Eternal Life to you." The arrow pierced right home. She went to her room and accepted Christ. Two days later when back in London, he received this telegram: "Got the smallpox badly–Dollie."

C. T. got gradually fitter, but not Mrs. Studd, and there did not seem much hope of a return to China. C. T. and his mother had always been greatly devoted to each other, and she would not hear of them living anywhere but with her. In other ways also the Lord wonderfully provided for them. One, whom they had never met before their return from China, constantly sent them large cheques ; and when he very suddenly died, the Lord moved another to send them regular gifts for many years. They proved what all prove who put God to the test, that He never fails those who trust Him. Neither they nor their children throughout this period or the remainder of their lives ever once lacked the necessaries of life.

Then a new opening came. The revival which had started among the students when C. T. and Stanley Smith visited Edinburgh had spread across the Atlantic. The connecting link had been C. T.'s brother, J. E. K. At Moody's invitation he had crossed to the States after the Seven had sailed for China, and there toured the Universities, telling the story of the Seven. Students in the U.S.A. caught the fire, and two of their number began the St udent

Volunteer Movement, with remarkable results. Hundreds were enrolled, and out of it grew in turn the worldwide Student Volunteer Missionary Union, and then the Student Christian Movement. One other outstanding result of that visit had been the conversion of a student who was destined to have a worldwide influence, John R. Mott.

Now came C. T.'s turn. In 1896 he was invited across. He remained eighteen months. The time was simply packed with meetings, sometimes six in a day; indeed, it was too packed, and he was very tired towards the end. When they gave him a free hand, he seldom spoke under one hour, and sometimes as much as two. His spare time was an endless succession of interviews with students. The way he dealt with student inquirers is an education in the way to bring young men and women right through into assurance of Salvation and the fullness of the Holy Ghost. We can only just pick out an instance here and there from his letters. "Knoxville. June 24, 1896. I have had such a good day today, early up and a quiet time for most of the day and the Lord has been opening up the Word. I feel I have been such a backslider; I always seem to get so lazy when I go home. Do pray for me. I find I do not one bit understand the Word unless I spend much time early with Him and then He makes the page to shine. I am generally awake and reading and praying soon after 4 a.m."

"Lincoln, Nebraska. Dec. 5 . Hallelujah! J u s t caught a fish. I was coming back here to the hotel when a student met me and began to talk to me in the street about his soul. We stood and talked. He was miserable, and began to have tears in his eyes, so I said, 'Come to my room and do business with the Lord.' He came, gave himself utterly away to Jesus, saw that Jesus must have taken him because He can't lie, thanked, asked for the Holy Ghost, received by faith, on the same principle that Jesus can't lie: He must give the Holy Ghost to him who asks. Then I turned to him and told him he was to let the Holy Ghost do the work in him and through him. He seemed to understand a bit, but face unchanged, dark and unhappy. I said to him, 'Does a man generally keep a dog and then go barking himself"?' He laughed, his face changed in the twinkling of an eye and he burst into praising God.

'Oh, I see it all now, I see it all now' ; and then he laughed and rejoiced and prayed all at the same time." " Minneapolis. Jan. 14, 1897. After tea had meeting at 7.30 to 8.30. The Lord blessed the students and some others, but I heard that the President thought I used too much 'slang.' Anyhow, it doesn't seem to have hurt the Lord much, for that night young A. asked me to go a walk with him; we talked over his case and he decided on a full surrender, which he completed in my room that night a grand time. Then again next morning had interview with wounded birds and had a grand time with two boys. Then again at 2 p.m. had another interview with a volunteer, who, I found, had never been converted and so could not do work for Jesus, and was under distress and condemnation, but he came most gloriously into the light. He received the gift of Salvation, surrendered and received the Holy Ghost. Oh, t he Holy Ghost came right down upon us and it was glory, glory everywhere around us and in us.

"I hear they have had blessed times at Bloomington College, where I was in November. Since my visit 23 conversions among the students."

"Ripon College, Wisconsin. Jan. 21. I had a very full Sunday. First meeting at 9 a.m. with the Y.W.C.A. girls. The Lord was very present and opened one's mouth. Then I had to proceed to M.E. Church for 10.30. Had a rare good time, speaking for just about an hour. At 4.30 p.m. had a rattling students' meeting, the place full and they were most interested: I did not finish till near 6. At 7 had to speak at a Christian Endeavour Young People's Meeting, and then at 7.30 a united meeting of the four chief churches in the town, Baptist, Presbyterian, Methodist and Congregational. I spoke for 91 minutes."

"Nicholasville. Feb. 23··· Soon after I reached the hotel a theological student came and wanted to speak to me. We talked a long time, and at the end I found he had never received Salvation as a gift; he was trying to buy it or earn it by good works. So when I had put it to him aright, he just beamed all over, got on his knees and received the gift, gave himself as a gift to God and received the gift of the Holy Spirit. It was grand and he was so thankful.

"Lewisburg, Bucknell College. April 5. Had a splendid students' meeting at 6.30. The Lord was greatly with us. After some hymns and a prayer I spoke for about 30 minutes ; then all got on knees, and one after another gave themselves to God in such sentences as 'Lord, take me as I am,' 'I will go with Thee, Lord Jesus.' There must have been a score of them. Oh, surely that is the sweetest music that can ever be heard by any ears, and if sweet to us, how much sweeter to Jesus. Afterwards I got them to sing a hymn:

"The cleansing blood I see, I see,
I plunge, and oh, it cleanseth me.

"[In a letter to C. T. from Indianapolis, June 16] I want to tell you and give God the glory, that your visit in Indiana was used with abundant results. DePaw has had a revival which resulted in the conversion of 40 men. I was at Hanover recently ; they followed your visit with special meetings, a number of men were reached, among them some who had been considered the hardest cases in College, the whole tone of the school is changed."

Among his letters C. T. sent home a cutting giving various complimentary details of his life. His comment in the margin is, "This is the kind of rot they write in the papers. One day a man got up and said something like this just before I spoke, so I got up and said, 'If I had known this was going to be said, I would have come at ¼ hour late. Let's get and wash it out in some prayer.' "

"Knoxville Students' Conference, June 21. After I had returned to my room [writes C. T.] and just upon 10 p.m., in rushed a student and said, 'Since hearing you this morning, I have thought of nothing but hell, because I have not and cannot surrender,' (though I had not spoken of hell or anything like it). I said 'Why can't you surrender?' 'I don't know.' 'Do you want to?' 'Oh, yes.' 'Well, do it now, get down here on your knees and tell God you will give Him all.' 'I think I may have been unwilling to do as He told me.' 'Well, are you willing now to leave all sin and do His will?' 'Yes.' 'Then just give yourself to Him.' He knelt down and after a short time gave himself right up and immediately arose with such a joyful, beaming face and said, 'It's all right now.' He needn't have told me.

"Spirituality is much needed here, there is a great lack of it, too much laughing and chaffing, not a real deep spiritual power. And why? Because they are afraid of it. Fancy! They are afraid of minds getting strained, and so instead of giving them fewer meetings, they dilute with the ditchwater of nonsense too often.

In the afternoon I read and prayed: the others had gone on a boat for an outing and ice creams. Missed tea on purpose, and took the evening meeting. We had a great time. I spoke for an hour and 40 minutes. The fellows were quieter at the end than even at the beginning. The Lord was with us in power. Many stayed to speak or arrange interviews. Two came that night. One medical student, uncertain about being a volunteer; he has a mother and sister dependent on him, and he wept as he spoke of leaving them. I took him over the old ground. He saw the love of God, surrendered and left bright. I don't tell these fellows to volunteer, I tell them to surrender to God and to go away rejoicing in Him, and He will in His own way make all plain. Oh, there is no joy in the world like being used of God to bless others. The place is now just on fire, and one so regrets now that this break didn't come earlier, as it might have done, had the talks been more spiritual and appealing to the heart.

"Next day I had interviews all the afternoon and evening, a real glory time. One man told me as I began to probe him–for something seemed wrong–that he had been converted, was saved and was an Episcopalian. So I said, 'Are all your sins forgiven?' 'No, not all.' 'Ain't it rather dangerous to have any unforgiven?' 'I suppose it is.' 'Do you want them forgiven?' 'Yes.' I explained a bit to him and then he got down on his knees to confess; he was going to confess out aloud to me the sins he had committed, but I stopped him and said I didn't want to hear them, but that he had better tell them to God. So we knelt and he told them to God, and then out aloud he asked for forgiveness. I asked, 'Has He forgiven you?' quoting, 'If we confess,' etc. 'Yes, He has.' 'Then thank Him.' And he did so. Then he surrendered and asked for the Holy

Ghost, and thanked and afterwards when I had prayed, he rose up with tears in his eyes, pressed my hand and said, 'I never had such an experience as this before.' Glory be to God ! You can imagine I went off to supper as full of joy as a gas balloon. Oh my, these souls are indeed more than diamonds, I'd far sooner save one soul than be Queen Victoria."

"As I came away from supper a man with such a sad face came to me and wanted an interview. He told me he could not conquer a certain kind of sin. I took him off to my room.

He said he was a Ministerial Student, he had been converted but had lately fallen into this sin and it had mastered him. We talked long, he loathed it and wanted to quit. He saw his own utter impotence. I said, 'Have you surrendered?' 'Yes, I have, yet sinned again.'

'Have you since that asked forgiveness?' 'No.' 'Well, that comes first.' 'Will you do so now?' 'Yes.' We got on our knees and he confessed and asked forgiveness and received it and that consciously; then he again made a full surrender, and I said, 'Now ask for the Holy Ghost.' But he did not understand and argued about the Baptism of the Holy Ghost, while we were on our knees. I showed him the difference between Apostles before and after Pentecost. He owned that if he was filled with the Holy Ghost, he would not be committing the sin. At last he asked to be filled, and then I prayed and asked God to take out the desire and let it no more enter in: oh, his whole heart went out into it, and he got up anew, and said, 'I know, for I feel He has given me the victory.' So I said, 'Then get down on your knees again and thank Him,' and he did. His face had before had despair as black as night written on it, but now it was all changed. He was in tears of joy and went away rejoicing.

"[Next day] Last night I saw and had a talk with him. He is the one who had become a slave to a sin. He said it was all right, God had given him complete victory and he was a new being: we went under a tree and kneeling down, had some prayer.

"H. was next, and the Lord led me in a strange way. After a bit he said he was saved, sins forgiven. 'Why do you think so?' 'Oh, I feel so.' 'What makes you feel so?' 'Oh, I am trying to make Jesus my example.' 'Oh,' said I, 'then you are quite sure to be damned,' It slipped out before I knew it, and it did the Lord's work, for the fellow was perfectly astounded and asked me again and I repeated it : it so astonished and convicted him, that he asked in the exact words of the Philippian jailer, 'Then what must I do to be saved?' So I showed him. After a while he got down and confessed, received salvation as a gift, then surrendered and asked for the Holy Ghost, and went away quite different."

"Monmouth, Nov. 19. Had a splendid time all yesterday with souls, interviews all day long, and in the last case a backslider who had fallen into deep sin. He looked as black and sullen as despair, but a three hours' fight gave complete victory. I had him an hour and then had to rush off straight to a meeting: another student took him on till I came back, and I returned two hours afterwards to find he had got the victory just before. You should have seen his face, oh, so bright, it was marvellous. "After tea the leader of the College Y.M.C.A. came and made a full surrender, asked for the gift of the Holy Spirit and went away knowing he had received, so bright and believing and set on doing personal soulsaving work. There is such a lack of this. It seemed the same tale every place, spiritual darkness because of this not doing personal work. You should have seen the shining face yesterday of the President of the College Y.M.C.A. He had been a Christian two years and had never won one soul. He won his first the night before at my meeting, and yesterday he said he had never been so happy and never believed he could be so happy—too happy to sleep.

"The same evening S. came round and said he had been asked to speak at chapel next day. The Lord at once seemed to tell me that I should have to speak, but I said nothing. God stopped S. speaking ten minutes or more before the end of the time; he could not think of another word, though he had prepared to speak for 25 minutes; every word left him and he had to sit down. I was thereupon asked if I would speak, although I was sitting at the back of the building. I walked up as fast as I could lay legs to the ground and began right away. I prayed first just these words, "Oh, Lord, make my tongue go as fast as my heart, for Jesus Christ's sake,' and He answered abundantly. I spoke with all the gusto of making a century at cricket against the Australians. Oh, it is so good to know the Lord is with one.

"Then S. came to my room with me for a talk. He came right full out, confessing, surrendering and receiving the Holy Ghost. Oh, such a change as you cannot understand, he is unrecognisable ; we are just about drunk with the Spirit. Oh, such freedom in prayer. We just laughed and thanked and prayed before God.

"God has made things so plain to me and enables me to put it plainly to others. Here is the gist of what I tell them. Assurance of salvation depends on the fact that Jesus paid the penalty of your sin, not on any feeling of yours. As Christ died for you, you belong by rights to Him. After further explanation I say, 'Will you not in a practical business way on your knees yield yourself and all to

Jesus?' 'Yes.' Then he or she does it, and I ask if Jesus has accepted them. If they do not know, I simply ask if God is a liar, which at once produces the required assurance, as it is impossible for God to have lied. Then I tell the inquirer to ask in one sentence for the Holy Ghost, and he does it. Then I ask, 'Has He been given?' By the same method the answer comes back 'Yes'; then I tell him to thank God for (I) having accepted him (2) having given the Holy Ghost. Then I say, 'Don't worry or fret, or think, or try, but just be careful for nothing, only trust and obey His voice. Rejoice and be glad in Jesus always. The feeling will come in due course, but it is a fact that God has given the Holy Ghost. Do not hinder God by helping Him, but quit hindering Him.' They come longfaced, and go away sparkling and beaming."

CHAPTER XII

SIX YEARS IN INDIA

"THAT church is a place to be avoided unless a man means to get converted." This sounds like the early church at Philippi or Ephesus; but it is still the same today, when preachers believe in the Holy Ghost. The remark was made about Mr. Studd's church at Ootacamund, South India, where for six years, from 1900 to 1906, he went to be Pastor of the Union Church.

From the time of his conversion C. T. had felt the responsibility upon their family to take the Gospel to India. It had been his father's dying wish. C. T. had written to his mother from China :

"George told me of how the people know the name of Studd in Tirhoot (North India) and how they flocked to see him when he was there: but what have they seen? Studd the indigo planter, Studd seeking wealth, but never Studd seeking the salvation of the souls of natives. Are they not going to see Studd the ambassador of

Jesus Christ?"

Now he was given the chance of going himself. Mr. Vincent, his father's old friend, urged him to fulfil his father's wish and go out to Tirhoot and hold meetings amongst the planters, promising to make all: the arrangements. C. T. accepted and was at Tirhoot for some six months. He then received the offer of becoming Pastor of the independent church at Ootacamund under the auspices of the AngloIndian Evangelization Society.

His work lay among all types: the planters in the outlying districts of Mysore and Madras, among whom he took long and arduous journeys; the population of "Ooty," European and Eurasian; the soldiers in the neighbouring Soldiers' Home, with whom he was tremendously popular; the officers and their families, and Government officials, who crowded to this lovely hill station in the hot months, including the Governor of Madras and his wife, Lord and Lady Ampthill, of whom they saw a good deal, as Lord Ampthill was an old Etonian. They were often invited to Government House. This gave them many opportunities of getting into personal touch with people who rarely had spiritual things put simply and naturally to them. Lord Ampthill was very kind to C. T., and when he was so bad with asthma, took him and Mrs. Studd to stay at Government House, Madras, and arranged for his own doctor to perform a special nose operation on him. During this visit C. T. also met Lord Kitchener, who, when introduced, said, "Ah, yes, of course we all know C. T. !"

As usual he went straight out for souls, both at the Union Church and amongst the planters, and found responsive hearts in unlikely quarters. A good number professed conversion, and Mrs. Studd once wrote home, "I don't think a week passes here that

Charlie does not have one to three conversions." But the pull of the world was very strong in this popular station, and only those stood who really went the whole way with God, and who got a salvation which took the love of the world out of their hearts.

One of the first he led into assurance of salvation was the wife of a colonel. Then there was an old Etonian who had been a contemporary of his and rowed in the Eton Eights. C. T. joined a cricket tour in order to get opportunities of holding meetings with the soldiers at night, after they had played the regimental teams. His old form returned to him, and in 1904 he made two double centuries, a feat which had only been performed once previously in Indian cricket. During the tour he became especially friendly with a Christian political officer, Col. W. G. Grey. As an illustration of the true unity in Christ of those who may be poles apart in the outward church, Col. Grey tells how he persuaded C. T. to call on the Bishop of Madras. On his return he asked him how he had got on. C. T. replied, "Rather stiff at first, but when he found that I loved the Lord Jesus Christ as he did, it was all right then!" Lord Curzon, the Viceroy, had a long chat with him when on a visit to Ootacamund, and asked him to come as his guest to the Delhi Durbar to represent India in a match against an Eleven from England.

An outstanding conversion was that of a chief clerk in the Military offices. He had not opened his Bible for twenty three years, but was persuaded to go to the Union Church by his little son, who said, "You must come and hear Mr. Studd. Why, he talks about bread and butter in the pulpit," referring to some incident which C. T. had told to illustrate how the Lord supplies everyday needs. He went, and went again. Then he wrote Mr. Studd, "Each Sunday at the Union Church I get hit harder and harder. This last week I felt

I had to make my decision. There was a big fight between God and me and the devil. Thank God, He won." The change was so marked that his native boy's comment was, "What has happened to the master? He always talking plenty swear words : now he only doing plenty Church work," alluding to the family prayers he had started in his home.

'Among the planters too he had encouraging results, especially through personal dealing, but the difficulty was to follow up the work in the outlying districts. His simple direct methods of giving the Gospel reached their hearts; as he wrote to his wife: "'Why do not others,' say they all, 'put it as plain and simple and straight as this?' "

But all this work was carried on against tremendous odds. Not only in India, but for some years previously, C.T. had been a martyr to asthma. He hardly slept except between 2 and 4 a.m. Night after night he was sitting up in a chair fighting for his breath. Charlie is a wreck," wrote Mrs. C. T., "and almost the slightest movement brings on asthma." Yet this was the man who by faith stepped out later into the heart of Africa and lived there for eighteen years. No wonder even his own wife was opposed at first. No wonder afterwards her favourite phrase was "The God of the Impossible." Mrs. Studd and the four girls, Grace, Dorothy, Edith and Pauline, the eldest of whom was then twelve had followed him to "Ooty." It was an ideal place for the girls, and they spent happy years there. Their father taught them riding, and at the same time, courage, which he considered one of the greatest of all virtues. He put them on a pony which pitched each one in turn over his head the first time they rode him. Mrs. Studd remonstrated, but he answered, "You must not inculcate fear into them, or they will be cowards.

They must learn to ride Gamecock, for if they master Gamecock, they'll ride anything after."

All four decided for Christ while in India, and C. T. describes the unique Baptismal Service :

"The time for our leaving India came in sight, and the girls wanted to be baptized. We belonged to the Union Church, of which I was Pastor, so we were neither Church of England nor C.M.S. The church man was high, the missionary was low, and somehow we must have fallen between the two stools, or underneath. Consequently I had to baptize the children myself. But where? There was no satisfactory place. However, the vision came, and we were not disobedient to it. I ordered the gardener to dig up one of the biggest flower beds to a substantial depth, then I went down to one of the commercial houses and purchased the biggest zinclined case I could find and fitted it into the flower bed. Meanwhile I stood outside the box in a similar hole, but without water. The weather was very cold, so the morning of the baptism saw a stream of black boys carrying kettles and saucepans of all dimensions, full of hot water, which they emptied into the box. They had to keep at it pretty persistently, because at the last moment we found that there was a leak. We had a good crowd up to our house; the preliminary meeting was in the drawing room. We sang and prayed. Amongst the company was an old C.M.S. missionary and his wife, whose faces fairly beamed, for they also were lovers of the girls. There was also a Baptist missionary and his wife, Miss Amy Carmichael, and sundry other missionaries. I got one of them to ask what questions he liked of the girls, one by one. They came through the ordeal all right, and then we went to the flower bed. One by one they went in and came out again, while appropriate singing was going on. I am afraid my girls, trained in such an extraordinary school as ours, where my wife was headmaster and I was matron, imbibed the spirit of fun that possessed us. At any rate, after the ceremony the girls got it off on me that I had baptized two of them with the wrong names. Once more we went to the drawing room, and there partook of the Lord's Supper in what I suppose people would call a very unconventional way. The C.M.S. missionary said he had never enjoyed a Communion Service more. I always think that the essence of a good dinner or breakfastparty is not the tablecloth, nor even the nature of the food, but the company. I think precisely the same concerning the Lord's Supper."

Only one more thing needs to be added about their stay in India, and that was that C. T. never moved from his attitude of dependence upon God alone for the supply of all needs, although he received an allowance from the AngloIndian Evangelization Society, for when he accepted he wrote to his wife:

"Only now let us remember once more that God is to be our portion, and that knowingly and willingly we trust our lives and those of our children to Him; if He fails, we are done for; but how can He fail? It is blasphemy on my part to suggest such a thing. Glory be to Him for allowing us this second privilege ; only it must be trust in Him and in Him only, not one little bit in any Society; if they pay our expenses, well *and* good, but I am not going to trust in God and them, I shall trust only in God, and so will you."

CHAPTER XIII

A MAN'S MAN

Their return home in 1906 brought them yet another proof of God's faithfulness. The girls needed schooling, of which none was to be obtained at "Ooty." A boarding school would be best, but how could the fees be paid?

Eighteen years before, this young couple had gone to the uttermost limit of surrender to God. They had staked all on God's faithfulness; they knew that unless the Lord supplied their need, they would have no hope of giving their children as good an education as they themselves had enjoyed. But they believed God, and now the time to prove His faithfulness had come. They committed the matter to Him, and this is what He did. He gave the girls exactly the education which their father and mother would themselves have chosen for them, if they had the means to do it. He moved someone to send three of them to one of the best girls' schools in the country, at Sherborne, and to see them through their whole education, while they lived with their Granny for the holidays, and three of them to finish their education at Lausanne. Wonderful though this provision was, it would have been as nothing to their parents, if it had not been accompanied by the one great blessing that really mattered, the salvation of their souls. Two years later C.T. wrote :

"It is a great joy to see all my girls right out on the Lord's side. For that alone I feel I owe the Blessed Saviour every drop of blood and affection in body and heart. I wish I could be like Him. He was clad with zeal as with a cloak."

Ministers and workers among men now seemed to have awakened up to their golden opportunity of using an outstanding converted sportsman to reach men. Y.M.C.A.'s, Brotherhoods, Police Institutes, Wesleyan Central Halls, booked and rebooked him. In those two years, 19068, he must have spoken to tens of thou sands of men, many of whom never went to a religious service, but were drawn to hear him by his sporting reputation. He gripped and stirred his great audiences to their depths, and many were the decisions for Christ. His method of speaking dead straight as man to man, no mincing matters, using the ordinary language of the people, coupled with his humour, made a tremendous appeal to men. A Birmingham newspaper, for instance, which had a reputation for speaking slightingly of missionary and religious work, surprised its readers by the following comments:

"Mr. Studd is a missionary to emulate. And so all that band of college men for Handsworth thought as they cheered him to the echo, this man with the red tie and slim athletic body and the young face. After more than twenty years of harness he is bubbling over with life and humour ; no pessimism about him, no luke warmness; he loves and he follows, he teaches what he believes, he keeps a brave sunshiny face through all. No subtleties appear to puzzle him; faith is as brave as his speech is clear and straight."

An instance of the way he started a talk to men was the following at a business men's luncheon: "Gentlemen, you've had a rich dinner, you will be ready for plain speaking. I am not going to tickle you with a pulpit or academic display of language. I shall speak in ordinary language, in that which we are all accustomed to use when engaged in the real battle of life or in heart to heart talking. I once had another religion, mincing, lisping, bated breath, proper, hunting the Bible for hidden truths, but no obedience, no sacrifice. Then came the change. The real thing came before me. Soft speech became crude salt. The parlour game with the nurses became real cricket on the public ground. Words became deeds. The commands of Christ became not merely Sunday recitations, but battle calls to be obeyed, unless one would lose one's selfrespect and manhood. Assent to creed was born again into decisive action of obedience. Orthodoxy became reality. Instead of saying 'Lord, Lord,' in a most reverent voice many times and yet continuing deaf to the simplest commandments, I began to look upon God as really my Father and to rely upon Him as a real Father and to trust Him as such. Instead of talking about fellowship, I enjoyed it. Instead of being unnatural and constrained, I became natural and unconventional. I talked of God and Jesus Christ as Real Living Personal Friends and Relations. They have never chided me for it. If a man is willing to obey and sacrifice, he soon learns what is the blessed reality of the fellowship of God's Son Jesus Christ familiar and social intercourse. In other words I dropped cant and ceremony and became a Christian. Reverence, I observe in the New Testament, is not apparent politeness and manifest disobedience, but filial or childlike obedience, trust, and love."

He carried his evangelism on to the streets and into the houses of those who entertained him, instant out of season as well as in season. One instance was when at a certain country house in Dorset he led both host and butler to Christ. The host wrote later, "I have many a time thought of you and our talk. I don't think it is so much want of faith one has to contend with as one's own weakness, which makes it hard for the spirit of honesty to accept the 'free gift.' You will, I know, say 'Accept' (and I have accepted, thank God)…." And a few days previously C.T. had a letter saying, "The butler at Clyffe called on me and in course of conversation he told me of his taking up your hot water in the morning, with the result of acceptance Jesus Christ as his Saviour."

On another occasion he was staying with his great friend Doctor A.T. Wilkinson of Manchester, the greatest friend of the last years of his life. The doctor ordered a "growler" to take him to the station and told the cabby that his fare was C.T. Studd, the cricketer. The cabby said that he remembered seeing him play at the Old Trafford ground, the doctor told this to C.T., and the result was that the fare got up outside with the cabby, and tried to win him to Christ as they drove to the station. The cabby never forgot that drive.

CHAPTER XIV

THE GREATEST VENTURE OF ALL

WE are now coming to the last and greatest era of Mr. Studd's life–China, then India, and now the heart of Africa. The call came very suddenly, while he was still contemplating returning to India. He was in Liverpool in 1908, and saw such a strangely worded notice that it immediately caught both his attention and his sense of humour. "*Cannibals want missionaries*." "Why, sure they do, for more reasons than one," said he to himself, "I will go inside and see who could have put up such a notice as that." As he thought, it was a foreigner, Dr. Karl Kumm. But God was in that chance impulse, for in that meeting He called C.T. to the great work of his life.

"Karl Kumm had walked across Africa [writes C.T.] and was telling his experiences. He said that in the middle of the Continent there were numbers of tribes who had never heard the story of

Jesus Christ. He told us that explorers had been to those regions, and biggame hunters, Arabs, and traders, European officials and scientists, but no Christian had ever gone to tell of Jesus. *The shame sank deep into one's soul*. I said, 'Why have no Christians gone?' God replied, 'Why don't you go?' 'The doctors won't permit it,' I said. The answer came, 'Am I not the Good Physician? Can I not take you through? Can I not keep you there?' there were no excuses, it had to be done."

But ho w set about it? He had no money. At fifty years of age, after fifteen year of illhealth, how could he face tropical Africa? Karl Kumm's first suggestion was that they should cross Africa together from the Niger side, and this was agreed to; but, as C.T. afterwards said to Dr. Wilkinson, "This was the only time that God agreed with the doctors; for, when I was, against doctor's orders, due to go, the Lord put me to bed with malaria, and plainly said 'No!' " The next plan was a journey of investigation to the Southern Sudan, a thousand miles south of Khartoum, in order to find out exact conditions. Karl Kumm had stressed the rapid advance of Mohammedanism in those regions and the urgency of planting a chain of stations to stem the tide. As C.T. presented this challenge and his willingness to pioneer the way, it was taken up by a group of business men, who formed themselves into a committee to back the project–but on one condition. He must be passed by the doctor. Then things came to a dead stop. The doctor's report was absolutely against him.

"Too much love is sometimes as bad as too much hate [wrote C.T.]. the committee refused to let me go unless I promised not to go south of Khartoum, through intimation they had received from the doctor that if I ventured south of Khartoum, I should never come back. On my refusing to give the promise, they declined to help me to go, withdrawing the funds necessary for such a purpose."

Penniless, turned down by the doctor, dropped by the Committee, yet told by God to go, what was he to do? "The only honest thing." Once more he staked all on obedience to God. As a young man he staked his career, in China he staked his fortune, now he staked his life. A gambler for Go d! He joined t he ranks of the great gamblers of faith, Abraham, Moses, etc. in Hebrews xi., and the true apostolic succession, 'Men that have hazarded (gambled with) their lives for the name of our Lord Jesus Christ" (Acts xv. 26). No wonder he once wrote, "No craze so great as that of the gambler, and no gambler for Jesus was ever cured, thank God !" His answer to the Committee was this, "Gentlemen, God has called me to go, and I will go. I will blaze the trail, though my grave may only become a stepping stone that younger men may follow." He carried out His Master's Word to the letter, 'He that shall lose his life for my sake and the gospel's shall find it." The next twenty years were to prove the truth of the last paragraph, "shall find it."

He was due to sail in about three weeks and had no money. What was he to do? The very next day he had a meeting in Birmingham, speaking on the same platform as Dr. Jowett. It had already been given out that he was sailing in a few weeks, and none knew of the crash of all his hopes from a human standpoint the day before.

"I landed on the platform without knowing what I could say under the circumstances. Whilst the Chairman was speaking, a sudden thought came. It was the voice of God. 'Why are you not

C.T. STUDD
In the heart of Africa, two years before he passed away

GRACE (MRS. MUNRO)

GRACE (MRS. MUNRO)

GRACE (MRS. MUNRO)

PAULINE (MRS. GRUBB)

THE FOUR DAUGHTER

going?' 'Where is the money?' I replied. 'Can you not trust Me for it?' was the answer. It was like the sun bursting through the clouds. 'Of course I can,' I replied. 'Then where lies the difficulty?' came the answer. The chairman ceased speaking, and I got up and spoke exactly as I should have spoken had the Committee not withdrawn the funds. The next day I went up to Liverpool to hold the week-end meetings at the Linnacre Mission. We had a good time. On the Monday morning when taking leave, a friend, who had been a complete stranger to me before that weekend, put into my hand ?10. Imagine my excitement and joy. I had to pass through Liverpool to reach London. On my way through I told the cabby to stop at the Bibby Office, and on the strength of the ?10, booked my passage to Port Said, wiring to the Committee what I had done. Of course the ?10 would not take me to Port Said, much less to Khartoum and a thousand miles south and back again, but God sent in supplies in a wonderful way, with the result that I went."

He sailed December 15, 1910. He had trodden the winepress alone, for even his wife did not approve, but the Lord stood with him and filled his soul with glory and with visions of the work which was to be. The very day he sailed, God gave him an amazing revelation. Just one man far past pioneering age, setting out on a forlorn hope with hardly a fellow Christian willing to back him, the most we might expect to hear is that the Lord assured him of the success of the venture; but, instead, the Lord gave him a staggering message.

"As I left Liverpool, on retiring to my cabin the first night, God spoke in a very strange fashion. He said, 'This trip is not merely for the Sudan, it is for the Whole Unevangelized World.' To human reason the thing was ridiculous, but faith in Jesus laughs at impossibilities."

There seemed absolutely no connection between this man's going to a corner of the Sudan and the whole unevangelized world. Yet now we look back over twenty years and we see that the Worldwide Evangelization Crusade, which was the outcome of his going, has already planted the Gospel in the hearts of three continents, Africa, Asia and South America, besides Arabia and West Africa. Can we not again learn the lesson of what God is waiting to do by the man who will utterly believe and obey Him? The actual promise which God give him, and the way he took it, he wrote to Dr. Wilkinson: "My soul is on fire to do the work of Christ. I seem to hear Jesus saying, 'Go over and possess the good land of the world. Every place your foot shall read upon (thank God I have large ones) to you have I given it.'" Meanwhile he wrote his heart out of cheer, comfort and encourage his wife, and doubtless these letters must have helped to show her that God was with him of a truth, and to make her later such an ardent fellow worker :

"Dec. 20, 1912. Somehow God tells me all my life has been a preparation for this coming 10 years or more. It has been a rough discipline. Oh, the agony of it! The asthma, what has not that meant, a daily and nightly dying! The bodily weakness! The being looked down upon by the world folk! The poverty! And have I not been tempted? Tempted to stop working for Christ! Doctors! Relatives! Family! Christians! Who has not declared I tempted God by rising up, and 'going at it' again? It has not been I, it has been Christ Who has carried me through; I know it. And now the Hill is won. It is like 'Albuera'–'600 immortal British soldiers stood unconquerable on the fatal hill.' Only this is a poor weak worm of a creature that God has chosen to put into the fiery furnace and wall with Him, and bring him out again. And now! Ah, yes, He seems to be pouring health and strength into me, and a burning, consuming desire to live, to live for Christ and men. Glory! Glory! Glory! It is Jesus, supreme. He is my chief love and my Chief. And now, Scilla darling, all this separation is for our good, and what is far better, it is for God's glory and Christ's honour. I believe this assuredly: (1) Your health shall be restored. (2) You shall become a bigger firebrand for Jesus than ever you have been, and a far greater power than poor weak I could ever be. (3) Our girls shall be white–hot Christian warriors, and to God be all the glory. I think, and think, and think, and all upon the same line–*A New Crusade*. Things simply surge through my mind and head, and God speaks to me every time I lie down, and assures me that He is going to do a wonderful work. Darling Scilla, you remember Shanghai? Well, those days are going to occur again, only on a magnificent scale. Oh, this New Crusade, it burns in my brain and heart. It must be."

"Marseilles, Dec. 23. Once again at the threshold of the greatest work for Jesus of our life and times, the doctors declare you weak and delicate, and more or less done for; and, humanly speaking, it is, I believe, a fact. But Jesus can give you back life and health, and has a grand work before you. You need the touch of Jesus. Will you not leave the doctors, who can never make you strong, and consult Jesus? Darling, go to Jesus and give yourself to Him; and I fully believe you shall go round the world with me winning thousands to Jesus. But there is no other way for you and me to live, than by faith in Jesus. T he doctors would have frightened me into my grave long ago, had I paid attention to them, but I live, and live by faith in Jesus and the power of God. You must do the same.

I am going forward, trusting in Him. There are big things ahead. Join with me in this Crusade. It is the lame that take the prey. It is when we are weak we are made strong. We must call the Christians forth to war. You shall be my right hand. You shall be a prairie fire. You shall be my spur to spur me on to greater things. We will fight while we live, and then He shall give us that glorious crown, and you shall wear it, not I. God bless you, my own love. I love you better in your old age than ever I did in your youth."

"Jan. 1911. Let us in our old age reconsecrate ourselves to Jesus. He has done so much for us. For 24 years. He has kept us going, and kept our girls and saved them. God grant that as a silver wedding present He may give us this noble work to do for Him in Africa. I fear we have often been cold and lukewarm in His service; let us finish this next 10 or 20 years of our lives together in His service, in the high places of the field. This is our finishing work for Jesus and the souls of men. Nothing else can be the coping stone of our lives. There is no other finish up for us worthy of Jesus, the Gospel, or ourselves: so you and I will do it–do it for Jesus–and others shall rise up and follow. God bless you, darling."

At Khartoum he had a delay of some weeks. As a great admirer of General Gordon, he was glad of the opportunity of seeing something of the scenes of his last days. He spoke several times in the English Church, at the invitation of Bishop Gwynne, the Bishop in Khartoum, his unusual presentation of the Gospel gripping some of his audience, and leading to the conversion of the son of a famous Scottish divine. He also held the first Mission in Khartoum, amongst the Battalion of Northumberland Fusiliers then stationed there. There was much blessing. The Sirdar, Sir Reginald Wingate, took much interest in the projected tour, for he was anxious that missionary work should be established in the Bahrel-Ghazal. He invited C.T. to dine at the Palace on several occasions. C.T. procured some dress shirts, but found them two inches short in the sleeve. So he cut off the cuffs and stitched them into the coat sleeves so that they just showed. But when he put the coat on, he found that "the links came in the wrong place ; they looked up at my nose instead of down at my toes" ; then he consoled himself by adding, "However, Lord Curzon always had his shirts made so, consequently they probably thought I was a regular dog of a swell!" On one occasion he sat next to a Mrs. Wherry, who said, "I was at the Cambridge v. Australian match at Cambridge in 1882 when you played and beat them. You made the winning hit to the boundary where I was sitting, and the ball rolled under my petticoat; I stooped down, picked it up and threw it back again, and have regretted doing so ever since. I ought to have kept it and had a silver band put round it and presented it to you."

Accompanied by Bishop Gwynne, he set off for the Southern Sudan. Here they were met by Archdeacon Shaw of the C.M.S., and the three on mule and on foot went two and a half months' trek through the Bahrel Ghazal. The road lay through malarial and sleeping sickness country, and was so hard on the animals that twentyfive donkeys died out of twentynine; but in spite of its being the rainy season C. T. was splendidly fit throughout the trek, until he got back to Khartoum, w her e he went down with a very severe attack of malaria. They found the people very needy, but very few. The C.M.S. were already operating on the upper reaches of the Nile. It seemed absurd to start a new mission, as the work could be done by the C.M.S. extending their operations to the tune of two or three stations; and this was the solution ultimately arrived at.

But while trekking, information of yet greater importance had come to their ears. They were told that beyond the Southern Frontier of the Sudan, in the Belgian Congo, there were vast masses of people as depraved and destitute as those they had seen, who had never heard of Christ. That information was the basis of another message from God to C.T., and a commission to press yet further forward.

"Going down the Nile, on the return journey to Khartoum, God again spoke. 'Dare you go back to spend the remainder of your days in England, knowing of these masses who have never heard of Jesus Christ? If you do, how will you meet Me henceforth before My throne?' That settled the matter. After such a word it was impossible to have the pluck to stay in England."

* * * * * *

Eighteen months later two men, one over fiftytwo and the other but twenty, were pushing their way into the interior of Africa, across the Frontiers of the Belgian Congo, into the very heart ? the first pioneers of the Heart of Africa Mission, which was the first advance of a far bigger Crusade.

C. T. had retuned from Khartoum aflame for this New Crusade, and had forthwith launched it . Among other places he had visited Cambridge and stirred the C.I.C.C.U.[2] to the depths with the challenge of the unevangelized world. men who are now leaders in Christian work received a new missionary impetus, such as Howard Mowll (Bishop in China, now Archbishop of Sydney), Arthur

2 The Cambridge Inter–Collegiate Christian Union.

Pitts (C.M.S. Secretary in Kenya), and Graham Brown (Bishop in Jerusalem). He wrote a series of booklets which were not only the foundation of the Crusade, but blazed with the passion of Christ for the lost, and have been a call to arms that has sent dozens of men and women to the foreign field. *The Shame of Christ, The Jehad of Jesus, The Chocolate Soldier*, are "the most stirring appeals in modern missionary literature," so said Dr. Eugene Stock, late Editorial Secretary of the C.M.S.

"We *should* go crusading for Christ [wrote C.T.]. We have the men, the means, and the ways steam and electricity and iron have levelled the lands and bridged the seas. The doors of the world have been opened wide for us by our God. We pray and preach; we bow the knee; we receive, we administer the Holy Communion of the Passion of Christ; we recite the Creed triumphantly; we are optimists everyone; we shout 'Onward Christian soldiers, marching on to war,' and then?···and then?··· we whisper, 'I pray Thee have me excused!!!'What glorious humbugs we are!

"Five hundred millions of heathen have not yet been evangelized, so it is computed! Yet our great Missionary Societies have reached high watermark, and if they have not already begun to retrench, are seriously thinking of doing so. Meanwhile, the heart of Asia, the heart of Africa, and well nigh the whole continent of South America, are untouched with the Gospel of Christ.

"Last June at the month of the Congo there awaited a thousand prospectors, traders, merchants and gold seekers, waiting to rush into these regions as soon as the government opened the door to them, for rumour declared that there is an abundance of gold. If such men hear so loudly the call of gold and obey it, can it be that the ears of Christ's soldiers are deaf to the call of God, and the cries of the dying souls of men? Are gamblers for gold so many, and gambles for God so few?

" 'My Montenegrins,' said King Nicholas, 'will henceforth spill their blood for their persecuted compatriots.' When shall God be able to say to the devil, 'Hast thou seen My Christians of today? No longer do they seek for gold or pleasure, for honours or ease, from henceforth My Christians will spill their blood for the love and cause of My beloved Son, and the salvation of the neediest of men.' Yes, when? When indeed shall we see a real 'Church Militant here upon earth?' "

He thus proceeded to outline the principles of the New Crusade. "Believing that further delay would be sinful, some of God's insignificants nobodies in particular, but trusting in our Omnipotent God, have decided on certain simple lines, according to the Book of God, to make a definite attempt to render the evangelization of the world an accomplished fact. For this purpose we have banded ourselves together under the name of 'Christ's Etceteras,' and invite others of God's people to join us in this glorious enterprise. We are merely Christ's nobodies, otherwise Christ's Etceteras. We rejoice in and thank God for the good work being carried on in the already occupied lands by God's Regular Forces. We seek to attack and win to Christ only those parts of the devil's empire which are beyond the extremest outposts of the regular army of God. Christ's Etceteras are a union mission; a Christian, and, therefore, an international brotherhood; a supplementary Worldwide Evangelization Crusade.

"Our method is to search and find out what parts of the world at present remain unevangelized, and then by faith in Christ, by prayer to God, by obedience to the Holy Ghost, by courage, determination, and supreme sacrifice, to accomplish their evangelization with the utmost despatch.

"The Head, the Commander, the Director of this Mission is the Triune God.

"David selected five smooth stones from the brook to polish off Goliath. We therefore have selected the following five to be the basis of our operations, to which everyone who joins must adhere:

"(1) Absolute faith in the Deity of each Person of the Trinity.

"(2) Absolute Belief in the full Inspiration of the Old and New Testament Scriptures.

"(3) Vow to know and to preach none other save Jesus Christ and Him Crucified.

"(4) Obedience to Christ's command to love all who love the Lord Jesus sincerely without respect of persons and to love all men.

"(5) Absolute Faith in the Will, Power and Providence of God to meet our every need in His service.

"The funds for this work shall be sought from God only. Nobody else shall ever be asked for either a donation or subscription. No collection for Etcetera Work shall be taken up at any meeting held or recognized by this Brotherhood. If we seek first the Kingdom of God and His righteousness, we have the Word of Christ that God will supply our needs. If we degenerate into seeking anything else, the sooner we cease to exist, the better for ourselves, for the world and for the cause of Christ.

"The Etcetera Evangelist must be a man of God and not a child of man. He is not the salaried servant of the Etcetera Committee. He is a servant of Jesus Christ with Whom he has settled terms of agreement already. He knows no other Master. He has not the ghost of a doubt about God supplying his need; he carries his chequebook with him always, and has no fear of the cheques being dishonoured. If death overtakes him on the battlefield, he knows such to be a special mark of Christ's favour, Who has thus honoured and promoted him sooner than he had any right to expect. As he looks to God to supply his needs, so also shall he look to God for his guidance and shall obey Him.

"Too long have we been waiting for one another to being! The time for waiting is past! The hour of God has struck! War is declared! In God's Holy Name let us arise and build! 'The God of Heaven He will fight for us,' as we for Him. We will not build on the sand, but on the bedrock of the sayings of Christ, and the gates and minions of hell shall not prevail against us. Should such men as we fear? Before the whole world, aye, before the sleepy, lukewarm, faithless, nambypamby Christian world, we will dare to trust our God, we will venture our all for Him, we will live and we will die for Him, and we will do it with His joy unspeakable singing aloud in our hearts. We will a thousand times sooner die trusting only in our God, than live trusting in man. And when we come to this position the battle is already own, and the end of the glorious campaign in sight. We will have the real Holiness of God, not the sickly stuff of talk and dainty words and pretty thoughts; we will have a Masculine Holiness, one of daring faith and works for Jesus Christ."

CHAPTER XV

THROUGH CANNIBAL TRIBES

THE parting from his wife seemed even harder this time. But she was now with him in making the sacrifice, although the harder part was to be hers, to remain at home, never knowing from month to month what news she would receive of her husband, separated from her by seven thousand miles. The Lord spoke to her and gave her the victory a few days before he left.

"That night before I went to bed [she writes], I had an experience. I sat down by the fire, and as I thought of all that was going to happen to me, I began to weep. I do not often weep; but I wept sore that night. Then I thought, 'This will never do. I shall be ill tomorrow, and unable to help anyone.' Going up in the train that day to Waterloo, I had been reading a book in which there were two references, one was Psalm xxxiv, and the other Daniel iii. 29. I had decided that in my first spare moments I would read those passages, so I opened my Bible. The very first words seemed almost to knock me down. The first was 'I, ' 'I *will,*' it means determination, it means grit, courage; 'I will *bless*' – I will make the Lord happy– and that was not to be attained by weeping; 'I will bless the Lord at all *times*' – now! And before I got to the end of the verse, the tears were gone, and I got to that point where I could say, 'I will make the Lord happy *now*.'

"Then I read on, 'I sought the Lord, and He heard me, and delivered me from all *my fears*.' 'This poor man cried, and the Lord heard him, and saved him out of *all his troubles*' ; and then the last was the most astonishing of all, '*He keepeth all his bones*, not one of them is broken'; and coupled with this promise I was given Daniel iii. 29, 'There is no God that can deliver after this sort. I just felt every fear was gone, all my fears, all my troubles, all that 'left alone' was going to mean, all the fears of malarial fever and the poisoned arrows of the savages; and I went to bed rejoicing. I just laughed 'the laugh of faith' that night. I rose from my knees and wrote the experience to my husband and posted it to Marseilles, through he had not yet left this country."

On the eve of their parting, in a flash of inspiration, C.T. put the thought of both their hearts into a sentence, and that sentence became the motto of the Crusade. A young fellow sat talking with them and remonstrated with C.T. He said, "Is it a fact that at fifty-two you mean to leave your country, your home, your wife and your children?" "What ?" said C.T., "have you been talking of the sacrifice of the Lord Jesus Christ tonight? *If Jesus Christ be God and died for me, then no sacrifice can be too great for me to make for Him.*"

Again on the platform, just before the train left, he scribbled on a piece of paper two lines of impromptu poetry which beautifully revealed the inward motive of their action, signed it and gave it to his friend, Capt. Downes:

> "Take my life and let it be,
> A hidden cross revealing Thee."

From board ship he wrote to his wife:

"Feb. I, 1913. Well, my darling, God was good to keep us so busy that last night. He knew I could not stand much, and so He engineered us right through and gave the glory in our souls. I shall ever picture you running up with the camera. I longed, but dare not, say goodbye or kiss again. I dared not. The tears came as I thought of your tears up there, and tears again of joy at the way He comforted you. Now let us thank Him in anticipation not only with our lips but by our lives. You little dream of how I know that you pay the greatest price, only I did not dare say so to you, but I do admire you, darling, and shall ever do so, and honour must ever be according to the magnitude of the sacrifice. Don't be anxious. The Lord will be Victor, and He will bring us into a wealthy place. I have never felt the power of God more since those Shanghai days. Truly this has been like the Seven going out. Goodbye, my darling Priscilla. We began risking all for God and we will end as we began, loving each other utterly and only less than we love Jesus."

In a letter to Dr. Wilkinson he told of the fire burning within him in characteristic style :

"The Committee I work under is a conveniently small Committee, a very wealthy Committee, a wonderfully generous Committee, and is always sitting in session–the Committee of the

Father, the Son and the Holy Ghost. "We have a multimillionaire to back us up, out and away the wealthiest person in the world. I had an interview with Him. He gave me a chequebook free and urged me to draw upon Him. He assured me His Firm clothes the grass of the field, preserves the sparrows, counts the hairs of the children's heads. He said the Head of the Firm promised to supply all our need, and, to make sure, One of the Partners, or rather Two, were to go along with each member of our parties, and would never leave us or fail us. He even showed me some testimonials from former clients. A tough old chap with a long beard and hard–bitten face said that on one occasion supplies had arrived and been delivered by black ravens, and on another, by a whitewinged angel. Another little old man who seemed scarred and marked all over like a walnut shell said he had been saved from death times untold, for he had determined to put to proof the assurance that he who would lose his life for the Firm's sake should find it. He told stories more wonderful than novels and Arabian Nights, of escapes and hardships, travels and dungeons, and with such a fire in his eye and laugh in his voice, added, 'But out of all of them the Partner delivered me.' He said gambling for Christ was the best game in the world. He said the compulsory rest cure was rather hard on him now with his gambling craze still there, but the Chief Partner commanded it, and said he must not be selfish and greedy about it, that he had a good long innings and made the highest score so far, and had better sit quiet a big, with pads off and coat on, and encourage the others.

"It did me good to see this old warrior. He was like a bit of redhot quicksilver, and–one felt scorched up with shame and ever since I saw him, and heard him, I have had a sort of pocket telephone inside, ringing me up and saying at intervals, 'Go it, old chap, go in for a slog! Your eye's in all right, and their bowling is getting weak. Take the long handle, only a few minutes till the stumps are drawn, Go it! Go it! Go it! Bravo! Now again!!!"

C.T.'s one companion was Alfred B. Buxton, son of his old friend of Cambridge days, Rev. Barclay F. Buxton. Alfred had just taken his degree at Cambridge, but gave up the remainder of his medical course to come straight out with him. Together they journeyed through Kenya and Uganda to the shores of Lake Albert.

"Many were the difficulties and obstacles in our path [writes C.T.]. We had not passed this way heretofore. We had no acquaintance with the language of the natives among whom we should be travelling for some months. Whilst as regards French, the language of the Belgian officials, I knew but a little 'dog' and Buxton a little 'cat' French, the small residue we had failed to forget of the meagre stock accumulated at school in days gone by. But we always interviewed officials together, and it was wonderful how often when the dog could not raise a bark, the cat was able to bring out a meow. Many were the lions in the way, all looking exceedingly fierce; however, we remembered that 'Christian' of old encountered lions, but as he dared to proceed in spite of them, he found they were invisibly chained. Some said, 'The Belgians will not let you in because you are British.' I replied, 'That remains to be seen, and I go to prove it.' Even the heroic Bishop Tucker gave it as his solemn opinion that we should be unable to successfully run the gauntlet of the many deadly fevers and dangers to which we would be exposed, and would never come out alive. Then we met the lion of fever. My companion was very young and not overstrong his 21st birthday had not yet seen the light. Being still in British East Africa, we had not yet approached the real fever zone, but down he went with an obstinate attack which confined him to bed for a week. However, faith in doing the reasonable only is but a 'bastard' ; the 'heir' is that faith which joyfully attempts the impossible in the will and by the power of God–so we proceeded.

"At Masindi there was a fire in camp which destroyed one of our tents and other useful things, and also we were met by another lion, a real man–eater this one, who has had many victims in the past. My companion received a cable from relatives, who had been assured by another missionary that he was far too young and wholly unsuitable for pioneering in Congo Land, dissuading him in the strongest terms from proceeding. The boy had to face perhaps the most difficult and trying question of a lifetime, one which has caused many to turn aside and lose an eternal weight of glory. To such as take counsel with flesh and blood the question is a holy terror, leading to a wrong and faithless decision. But to the loyal Christian there must be but one answer to the question as to which comes first– the Father in Heaven, or relations on earth. His decision to proceed was that of a true 'Man of God.' God has owned that decision in a very wonderful way. Many others of more mature age have entered the Congo, and been the victims of fever again and again, but this stripling of faith during the next two years never had an hour's fever. God has also honoured those same relations by allowing them twelve months later to send another cable, this time to express their joy at the decision of a younger brother[3] to come and join us in Congo Belge."

---

3 George Buxton, who was due to start when war broke out. He joined up and was killed in the Air Force in 1916.

A three days' forest trek from Masindi brought them to the shores of the Lake Albert. "This morning we arrived at the foot of the hills on the East of Lake Albert and looked across at the hills on the other side, the Belgian Congo, our promised land. Can you imagine our feelings? It was a lovely sight, and there, sure enough, was the pillar of could above them." They crossed the Lake and another lion had his mouth shut, for they had a good reception from the Belgian Official, and were allowed to enter the Congo. That night, their first in Congo territory, they camped on the Lake shore :

"Dark came on and we had porridge for supper and a turn round in the bush to try for a buck, as we had precious little food. At dusk the mosquitoes and lake files were a perfect pest.

"I slept out in the open with the net, but had to go inside under the tent during the night because of rain. The files provided a treble to the grunt or barking of the crocodiles, the Lake was only 20 yards from our tent. I had never thought crocodiles made any noise before. It was not altogether nice to have them so close, and I took the precaution to keep a good fire burning between my bed and the Lake.

"I know I am God's [he wrote the first day in Belgain Congo], I know I only want His glory and the salvation of others, and I know He knows it. I never was better nor stronger for years and years, but best of all, I know God is with us. He talks to me, and His blessed Word means more than ever before, and halloos me on more and more, and makes me burn to dare and do for Him.

"Our journey lay through the fierce Balenda tribe [he continued], who had in the end killed Emin Pasha, of whom the surrounding tribes stood in unholy terror; it was difficult to obtain carriers, and the few that came with us only ventured to do so because they would be travelling with white men. A short while before this a white man had come across from Uganda. He was taken to the Chief Julu, who stripped his cloths off, beat him, and sent him back naked and ashamed. A little time after we had passed through them, an English elephant hunter was shot by a native of this tribe with a poisoned arrow in the shoulder and died.

'In these regions Mr. Buxton and I became separated one day from the porters; taking a wrong track, we travelled for over three hours up and down exceedingly steep hills with densely peopled villages; our cycles were mostly encumbrances. We had neither food nor money, and no knowledge of the language. Dead beat and with a terribly clamorous vacuum inside, we found ourselves up against an exceedingly tough proposition. Meeting a man with a basket full of raw maize cobs and sweet potatoes, we commandeered a small supply, but then were faced with the problem of how to pay for them. Necessity is the mother of revelation, and it came with a flash. Why do breeches have so many buttons? To be cut off and used as money in Central Africa, of course! A few sent off our friend as pleased as Punch, though how his wife would stitch them on his tightfitting black waterproof without causing him considerable pain is an enigma to which we have not yet found a satisfactory solution. At the next village a little 'dumb crambo' with that 'rara avis,' a man in clothes, proved an unqualified success; in a few minutes we had a fire, a cook, and much cheerful company. The cooking was commendably simple and unspoiled by any rich sauces. Having neither saucepan, gridiron, fryingpan nor even a paper bag, our chef pitched the food into the fire and pulled it out, done to a turn, half an hour afterwards; eating with considerable gusto, we soon found ourselves wit h revived strength, plus that comfortable after dinner feeling which frequenters of the Ritz are said to enjoy. A few more buttons settled the bill. Their field teeth declared our friendsinneed to be cannibals, but as both of us were lank, lean and tough, they were not tempted beyond what they were able to bear, so neither they nor we succumbed; hence we parted 'Dei gratia' the best of friends and amidst considerable applause.

"Kilo is a great goldmining centre, and there we were unavoidably detained for three whole months owing to transport difficulties. We became dwellers in tents and followed the simple life. With a tent, a bed, a box and a basin apiece, what more does anyone desire in the rainy season? While three stones in the open-air made a range and kitchen de luxe. You never know how much you can do without till you try. "Here I was permitted to sample the African fever so frequently as to know it by heart, but without any increase of affection. It was like being repeatedly ducked by the devil, and once I thought he had ducked me too much. But as each time on coming up one spluttered out, 'Sold again, old chap," he finally got so annoyed that he went and sat down in the sulks and left us alone. That big ducking was an ugly affair; the fever mounted, the weakness increased, all the medicines had failed, and the time for disappearing seemed to have arrived: the darkest hour brought a brilliant flash of memory: 'Is any sick, let him call for the elders of the church, and let them anoint him with oil,' etc. Thank God for the saving sense of aumour ; there was but one 'elder' and he was in his twentieth year; no matter, 'One day is as a thousand years.' But where was the oil? Neither salad, olive or even linseed oil did we possess! What's the matter with the lamp oil? What, kerosene? Why not? It is oil, and that is all the Book says, and we cannot afford to be narrowminded. The 'elder' brought in the lamp oil, dipped his finger, anointed my forehead, and then knelt down and prayed. How God did it I don't know, nor do I care, but this I knew next morning, that whereas I was sick, nigh unto death, now I was healed. We *can* trust him too little, but we *cannot* trust God too much."

They received their first mail from England here, and C.T. heard the news that he had become "The Pioneer Grandfather." His first grandchild, Ann, had been born; the child of his daughter Dorothy, who had married Rev. Gilbert A. Barclay. "I do thank God for His great goodness," wrote C.T.; "may God bless them both. I sort of tried to be anxious, but God always gave me peace and assurance about them."

"From Kilo to Arebi [continued C.T.], our track lay in the great Ituri forest, which Stanley passed through, justly famed for its precipitous and slippery paths, where the overhanging trees intercept the light of the sun, where you march to the tune of 'Drip! Drip! Drip! The drips are falling,' and where the forest denizens are the invisible pigmies. The forest was very beautiful in places, and sometimes it was like marching through an endless cathedral, the giant trees on either side representing the columns. We hardly saw a soul in the forest, and not a single animal. We could hear the African pheasants calling, but could hardly ever catch sight of them, and never near enough to shoot. Food was scarce, and we lived chiefly on baked banana and bread and tea. I have marched many tracks in my time, but I've never known one like this. It would have puzzled a goat to have got through. The hills were precipitous, the paths a succession of holes and treetrunks, and all religiously soaped by the devil night and morning to ensure their being slippery. With all our care, and with the aid of long sticks like Alpine climbers use, we came down pretty frequently. There was no thinking about it, one's heels were up and one's head down before you knew what had happened. The forest journey was one of eleven days, but we were halted for a fortnight midway in a forest clearing, for our porters refused to go further, and others were not forthcoming. The forest is neither good for fever nor rheumatism, but God saw to both all right as usual.

"From Arebi to Dungu the road was better and we were able to use our cycles a good deal. We had never seen Dungu, but the thought of it was sweet. There we should rest our weary feet and feel our goal had been reached at last, and there we should begin our work. The disappointment was hidden from our eyes, thank God, and once again we learned that the 'dis' is more rightly spelt

'His'. He had prepared a better thing for us. Our rest and headquarters were to be four days further west, plumb in the very heart of Africa, as the explorer, Dr. Goerge Schweinfurth, asserts Niangara to be. After a week at Dungu waiting for some of our porters, we left for Niangara. Three days down the Welle River in a canoe landed us there.

"At Dungu we had one great joy, that of meeting a real, true, faithful friend, though hitherto we had been perfect strangers–the Count Ferdinand de Grunne. Our debts to him were many and very great.

"If a man is faithful to God he is bound to lose some friends, but God always raises up others and truer ones to take the vacant places. The Court de Grunne was a friend indeed and a friend in need, not one merely in words, but also in deeds. No trouble was too much, no kindness too great for him to do. To him under God we owe our concessions at Niangara and Nala, and indeed, through his kind expressions and introduction to others on our behalf, the other twelve concessions also. He died a hero's death at Dungu just twelve months afterwards, hastening to go and fight his country's battles, though weak from a severe and prolonged attack of fever. Even on his deathbed he did not forget us, but dictated a letter which to me is worth more than it weight in gold."

So at last they had gained their heart's desire, and reached Niangara, the very heart of Africa, after nine months' arduous travelling and living mostly in tents, during which, as he said afterwards, "We got into so many tight corners, but always found God there, that we began to look out for, nay, even desire, tight corners to get into, that we might see how God would extricate us from them". It was remarkable how God led them on to this place, for it had not been their original plan. They had thought to start work at Feradje, ten days from Niangara; then when this door closed, at Dungu. Then the closing of that door had forced them on to Niangara. But now how thankful they were for these "disappointments." All around Feradje and Dungu the country is dreary miles of grassland from 5 to 18 feet high, with scanty population. But after crossing the river at Dungu the scene changes, vegetation becomes luxurious, grassland gives place to the giant trees and tangled undergrowth of the tropical forest, everywhere are little groups of grassthatched huts, surrounded by plantations of bananas and palm trees. They had entered the fringes of the great tropical forest which stretches for hundreds of miles to the south, and contains, though unknown to them at the time, the biggest population of the whole of Congo. Added to this, God had in His own wonderful way given them favour with this Roman Catholic

Government official of high standing, who not only directed them to all these strategic centres of population in this forest region, but enabled them to get concessions in them. The first stage of this venture of faith had been crowned with success beyond their dreams.

CHAPTER XVI

THE VERY HEART OF AFRICA

NIANGARA, the very heart of Africa, was reached on October 16, 1913.

"At the time we knew not whether our work would develop northwards or southwards [wrote Alfred Buxton]; but we are inclined, according to advice given us, to settle our Station four hours to the South, near the great Chief Okondo's village. Then at the beginning of December, Mr. Studd began to feel very strongly that we must have a place in or near Niangara as a Headquarters Station, and for the reception of parties. The idea grew, until we went out definitely in search of a site. The Government allotments, native population, and the lowlying bank of the river drove us farther out than we had expected, and we were just giving up the search, when we came to a beautiful grove of palm trees. We were so taken with the spot that the next day we went out and started to clear the bush. Alas, we had hardly begun, when the headman of a near village appeared and declared we couldn't have the land. Knowing that the native's consent was absolutely essential in the eyes of the Government, we were quite in despair, when the same native said he knew a better place to which he would guide us through the bush. It certainly was better! A fine spring, better elevation, good soil and an abundance of palms. That was *the* place. Next day we were out again and started to clear. Again the same story, only more natives, hotter words, and stronger gestures to show we were not wanted and could not have the land.

"Our next step was a trip five days south to Nala. The road was pretty poor, and we had to do a good deal of walking owing to the forest paths. It was very pretty, especially when we got near to Nala, where the road was lined with rubber trees and palms. The place is a splendid centre–Azandes to the West, Mangbettus to the East, and Medje and Mayogos to the South, not to speak of the Pigmies. Of course, all is forest. Medje and Nepoko, south of Nala, are the most densely?populated places in the Congo. It is wonderful how God has led us down to this country teeming with people, which would probably not have been discovered if we had remained on our original plans.

"Mr. Studd instantly applied to the Government for a concession at Nala. A few days after our return to Niangara, the Chief gave his consent to our occupation of the much–coveted site there, which promptly became ours. Thus God had forced us South, refusing to give us any concession in Niangara, until Nala had become His." Thus the two first stations were obtained. Immediate work was started at Niangara, clearing, planting and building. The first Mission House was up in a few weeks at the cost of £6, and was named "Buckingham Palace." While there C.T. had a narrow escape from a snake.

"God's protecting hand in over us. This morning we had just finished breakfast when the 'boys' came saying, 'There is a snake in your bed!' I went and found underneath my blanket a thin green snake, which the natives say is death if it bites you. I had slept with it last night. It was impossible for me not to remember that wonderful episode last January of Psalm xci and my having been given that Psalm at various places five times in two days just before I left. He had given His angels charge over me, and they had not fallen asleep."

The Government then asked Mr. Studd to go down to Nala to settle the boundaries of the new concession.

"This seemed God's call to a more extended trip to the South [wrote Mr. Buxton], which we had often discussed, right into the Ituri Province, which we heard was teeming with people. It was at a time when Mr. Studd was being much pressed to return home and take up the burdens there, and his own weakness seemed ample excuse for such a course. But God laid it heavily upon his heart that he must see that country before returning, and so down we went. What a country we found!

"Our tour was the greatest success we have had [writes C.T. to Dr. Wilkinson]. Nala concession was measured and made good to us, and I got a good photo of the final scene when the chiefs assembled, expressed their willingness and pleasure that we should occupy Nala, and attached their thumb prints in lieu of signatures. But after Nala was the most interesting time, for there we were breaking fresh ground. We passed through people who had been at war two months before; all carried bows and arrows, even the young children, but they were quite friendly with us. Ten years ago the first white man came among them with 35 soldiers to subdue the country. He was told one night that if he advanced the next day, he would be killed ; he advanced, and he and 33 of his men were killed, cooked and eaten. We saw the place where his bones ought to be. Less than five years ago the Medje Poste used to receive arrows nightly, shot by the natives into their settlement, and every new arrival had to run the gauntlet as he made his way along the track. Today they are quiet and friendly.

"Day after day they run along in front and behind our cycles, shouting, laughing and singing their chants ; you never heard such a din nor saw so great enthusiasm. From dawn till dark they are with us and around us. It was like an excited crowd surging round the pavilion at the conclusion of a great cricket match. One's head seemed like cracking, but it was only one's face that did that, through having to laugh and smile perpetually. Neuralgia, however, was a small matter when one's heart was so full of joy at having found the people God has sent me after during these years.

"We had searched and searched, and here they were. In 1911 on the Nile God said, 'You must go and see and find them, they are there across the Sudan boundary, you dare not leave them alone.' How the devil has fought for them, but God is stronger than he and has brought us two fools into the Den itself. Here were these people receiving us in the friendliest of ways. They would carry our cycles gratis, across streams or rivers, across broken, dilapidated, ramshackle bridges, and up and down gullies and ravines. They would lead us by the hand; men, women and children ran along with us ; one young lady held my hand one side pulling me up a gulley, and another elder one did ditto the other side ; one even put her arm around my neck ; and so we marched along amid the singing, laughing crowd, all as jolly as sandboys ; and of course I thought of what some folks would say if they could only have seen our triumphal march. 'Shocking! Scandalous! And he a missionary! Did you ever?' Well, we are both living happily ever afterwards! They didn't speak Bangala and we didn't speak Swahili, so we had to talk dumbcrambo. Fancy, there were hundreds of them all round us, sometimes 500, all running ; we often cycled fast too, but the women and girls ran and laughed and shouted as fast and boisterously and loudly as the men and boys. It was like a fox hunt at times, and I could only think of those lines :

"Yes, we'll all go a hunting today,
All nature looks smiling and gay,
So we'll join the glad throng,
Which goes laughing along,
Yes, we'll all go a hunting today.

"For we were never out of sight of a village, and every village poured forth its inhabitants to join the throng. It was a funniest thing in the world to see a woman catch the first sight of one riding along. Her face would express terror as though she had seen the devil ; then all of a sudden it would be changed to a huge, broad smile ; then she would drop her work and run after us, joining in the fun as only an African woman can.

"Well, here is our 'Eldorado.' Here is a land and a people to whom the Blessed Name had never been known throughout all time. Shall we leave them thus? We will not. We will sell our pottage and buy therewith our birthright to declare the glory of God to this people. They shall hear and hear to purpose by the Power of the Holy Ghost."

One more long trek was undertaken to Poko, five days north-west of Nala, and then another six days to Bambili. Both were good centres for opening work, and at both concessions were applied for and granted. In two years the Heart of Africa had been entered, surveyed, and four strategic centres chosen, covering some hundreds of miles and touching about eight tribes. How wonderfully God had prospered the men who dared to obey the Holy Ghost and leave the consequences with Him. Now the time to occupy and evangelize had come. News had already reached them of a party of five on the way ; so C. T. and his young companion separated, C. T. to continue the long trek for another three hundred miles beyond Bambili to the Congo River, then 700 miles to the mouth, and thus to England to enlist more recruits ; Alfred Buxton to meet the new party, open the work at Nala, and continue the reduction of the language to writing.

During C. T.'s absence the first baptismal service was held at Niangara on June 19, 1915, when twelve were baptized.

"When all had answered various questions satisfactorily [wrote Alfred Buxton], we went down to the river, and one by one Coles handed them down to me and I baptized them in the Name of the Father, Son and Holy Ghost. Afterwards we sang together, 'Oh, 'twas love.' It sounded particularly impressive and peaceful, and in strange contrast to the report of Coles' revolver, as he shot into the water to scare away the crocodiles."

At Nala where the first baptismal service was held six months later, each of the eighteen who were baptized carried back with him a large stone from the stream; they were set up in a heap in the middle of the station as a witness to their dedication to God. Those stones are still there, now around the grave of baby Noel Grubb, C. T.'s grandchild, who died at Nala, 1921, on his first birthday.

"Each of these Nala baptisms [wrote Alfred Buxton later] would make a stirring headline in *The War Cry* :

'Excannibals, Drunkards, Thieves, Murderers, Adulterers and Swearers enter the Kingdom of God.'

"At the meetings for the confession of sin, we had some remarkable testimonies : 'I have done more sin than there is room for in my chest.' 'My father killed a man, and I helped to eat him.' 'When I was three years old, I remember my father killing a man, and because he had killed my brother, I shared in eating the stew.' 'I did witchcraft from the finger nails of a dead man, and with the medicine killed a man.' "Each one is greeted, when they first come, with, 'What have you come here for? Because I tell you frankly there is not much money to be got here ; our men have enough to live on, but all we really care about is getting men to learn about God and to read His Word.' In spite of such a greeting, one and all have answered, 'We do not care a snap about money, what we want is God,'"

Later, one of the early converts, who was an old soldier, put his experiences of cannibalism to practical use in quelling a rebellion amongst some canoemen from a wild river tribe, who were paddling C. T. down the Aruwimi, by shouting out to them, "Get on with your work! Remember, in my time I have eaten better men than you." And there was no further trouble!

One of their greatest aids to widespread evangelism had been the discover y of a crude but invaluable commercial language called Bangala, used for trading purposes between the tribes, and between whites and natives. They at once saw its possibilities and determined to concentrate on it and develop it, and by this means get immediate contact with all the tribes of that region, rather than delay their evangelization for many more years by waiting until each tribal language had been mastered. Bangala became to them what Greek was to Paul, and Hindustani has been to the missionaries in India.

They persisted in concentrating on Bangala in spite of considerable criticism later on from other missionary bodies, who maintained that it was too poor a language to be a proper medium of spiritual truth. But they received unwavering support from the great language authority, Rev. R. Kilgour, D.D., the Editorial Secretary of the Bible Society, which later published the New Testament in Bangala, and from the language authorities of the Religious Tract Society, who published the first Tutor and Vocabulary in the language and later a large book of Old Testament extracts. That they have been magnificently justified in their persistence is proved by the fact that to day the Bangala Vocabulary, which was produced by Alfred Buxton, and the translations of the whole of the New Testament and about half of the Old Testament, are used by no less than six missions, including its old opponents, working among probably 100 tribes, and covering a thousand miles of territory between the Nile and the Congo.

* * * * * *

C.T. had many tests on his journey into Africa, but the severest of all came by news from home. Shortly after he sailed Mrs. C.

T. was suddenly taken severely ill on a journey to Carlisle. Her heart was found to have extended out several inches. For days she was only kept alive by stimulants, until, after a visit from Lord Radstock, and the prayer of faith, she turned the corner. But even then her recovery was but partial, and she remained an invalid with no likelihood of further improvement. The doctor's verdict was that she "must live quietly in every sense of the word for the rest of her life." She had to go to her room each night at seven and not come down the next day till lunch time.

No doctor's verdict, however, could now stop her from joining in the New Crusade. She had the example of her husband before her, and his victory of faith over all bodily weakness. More than that, she had God's call. She now knew that it was God who had led her husband to start the Crusade, and that He was calling her to the fight side by side with him. So, regardless of her condition, she took up the reins at the home end. At first she nominally kept to the doctor's instructions in hours of rising and retiring, but broke all rules in the amount of work she did. Later, as we shall see, she took the whole plunge.

From her bed and invalid couch she formed Prayer Centres, issued monthly pamphlets by the thousand, wrote often twenty and thirty letters a day, planned and edited the first issues of the *H.A.M. Magazine* in its original heart shape. Her daughters helped her in the work, Grace's husband, Mr. Martin Sutton, being the first chairman of the Committee until his sudden death a year later ; Edith and Pauline living with their mother and helping in various ways.

Consequently, when C. T. arrived home at the end of 1914, he found a properly established Headquarters at No. 17, Highland

Road, Upper Norwood, and the home end of the work being carried on vigorously.

Certainly the foolishness of God is wiser than men. In two years the heart of Africa had been pioneered by a grandfather and a physical wreck, while the home end of the Mission had been established by an invalid from her couch. Such was the foundation of the H.A.M. Exactly "according to plan," God's plan, which only requires one thing for its fulfillment, not education, nor talents, nor youth, nor strength, but *faith*. By faith Abraham··· by faith Moses··· by faith C. T. Studd···

For the last time on earth C. T. went up and down the homeland, urging and pleading with God's people to rise up and fight and sacrifice for perishing souls, with at least as much zeal and heroism as they were displaying in the Great War then at its height. He refused to spare himself. Seldom has any voice pleaded the cause of the heathen as his pleaded it. He was weak and wasted from his long travels. He had constant attacks of malaria. Sometimes he went to the platform with the fever on him, and preached his temperature down to normal. At Colwyn Bay, for instance, he wrote :

"Nov. 2, 1915. Hughes Jones, mine host, brought in a doctor, who forbade me to go out and speak that evening, and said that I must go home at once. I laughed and spoke for an hour and a half ; next day Carnarvon two hours ; then Bangor three meetings, and then Aberystwyth. Oh, these train journeys! So slow and so cold, but God is always there."

He took the magazine in hand and issued the most stirring appeals that pen could write.

"There are more than twice as many Christian uniformed

officers at home among peaceful Britain's 40 million evangelized inhabitants, than the whole number of Christ's forces fighting at the front among 1,200 million heathen! And yet such call themselves soldiers of Christ! What do the angels call them, I wonder? The 'Let'ssave Britainfirst' brigade are in the succession of the 'Ipray theehavemeexcused' apostles.

"Christ's call is to feed the hungry, not the full ; to save the lost, not the stiffnecked ; not to call the scoffers, but sinners to repentance ; not to build and furnish comfortable chapels, churches, and cathedrals at home in which to rock Christian professors to sleep by means of clever essays, stereotyped prayers and artistic musical performances, but to raise living churches of souls among the destitute, to capture men from the devil's clutches and snatch them from the very jaws of hell, to enlist and train them for Jesus, and make them into an Almighty Army of God. *But this can only be accomplished by a red-hot, unconventional, unfettered Holy Ghost religion*, where neither Church nor State, neither man nor traditions are worshipped or preached, but only Christ and Him crucified. Not to confess Christ by fancy collars, clothes, silver croziers or gold watchchain crosses, church steeples or richly embroidered altarcloths, but by *reckless sacrifice and heroism* in the foremost trenches.

"When in handtoband conflict with the world and the devil, neat little biblical confectionery is like shooting lions with a peashooter : one needs a man who will let himself go and deliver blows right and left as hard as he can hit, trusting in the Holy Ghost. It's experience, not preaching, that hurts the devil and confounds the world, because unanswerable ; the training is not that of the schools, but of the market ; it's the hot, free heart and not the balanced head that knocks the devil out. Nothing but forked-lightning Christians will count. A lost reputation is the best degree for Christ's service.

"I am more than ever determined that no ring nor limit shall be placed around us, other than that of our Lord Himself, 'To the uttermost parts,' 'To every creature.' I belong and will ever belong to 'The Great God' party. I will have nought to do with 'The Little God' party. 'The difficulty is to believe that He can design to use such scallywags as us, but of course He wants Faith and Fools rather than talents and culture. All God wants is a heart, any old turnip will do for a head ; so long as we are empty, all is well, for then He fills with the Holy Ghost.

"The fiery baptism of the Holy Ghost will change soft, sleek Christians into hot, lively heroes for Christ, who will advance and fight and die, but not mark time. Let us race to heaven ; an accident means dashing into the arms of Jesus–such accidents are God's choicest blessings. Don't be a luggage train.

"Fools would 'cut' the devil, pretending they do not see him ; others erect a tablet over his supposed grave. Be wise ; don't cut nor bury him ; kill him, with the bayonet of evangelism.

"Hugh Latimer was an inextinguishable candle ; the devil lit him, and ever since has been kicking himself for his folly. Won't someone else tempt the devil to make a fool of himself again?

"Nail the colours to the mast! That is the right thing to do, and, therefore, that is what we must do, and do it now. What colours? The colours of Christ, the work He has given us to do–the evangelization of all the unevangelized. *Christ wants not nibblers of the possible*, but grabbers of the impossible, by faith in the omnipotence, fidelity and wisdom of the Almighty Saviour Who gave the command. Is there a wall in our path? By our God we will leap over it! Are there lions and scorpions in our way? We will trample them under our feet! Does a mountain bar our progress? Saying, 'Be thou removed and cast into the sea,' we will march on. Soldiers of Jesus! Never surrender! Nail the colours to the mast!

"Such as look to Jesus become grasshoppers in their own sight, but giants in the estimation of the devil.

" 'Follow Me,' says Jesus, 'I will,' we reply, yet somehow forget that Christ pleased not Himself, deliberately made Himself poor to save others and became the first foreign missionary. We all pray to be like Jesus, yet refuse to pay the price. How can Dives be like Jesus?

"The crumbs of Dives are not a dainty dish to set before King Jesus. Try 'cake' for a change, and don't forget to put all you've got into it.

" 'But what if C.T. dies?' This frequent and foolish question must have its answer. Here it is from C.T. himself, 'We will all shout Hallelujah. The world will have lost its biggest fool, and with one fool less to handicap him, God will do greater wonders still. There shall be no funeral, no wreaths, crape, nor tears, not even the Dead March. Congratulations all round will take place. 'And I, if I be offered up, rejoice and congratulate you ; do ye also rejoice and congratulate me.'–Phil. ii. 17 and 18 (Lightfoot's Translation). The Wedding March, by special request. Our God will still be alive and nothing else matters. The first Heart of Africa Mission funeral will take place when God dies, but as that will not be till after eternity, cheer up all. Forward! Every man straight before him. Hallelujah! 'To die is gain.'

"Some wish to live within the sound
Of Church or Chapel bell,
I want to run a Rescue Shop
Within a yard of hell."

In July, 1916, all was ready for his return to Africa. A party of eight were equipped. They included his daughter Edith, going out to marry Alfred Buxton. The farewell meetings were fixed for July 14, "Don't forget July 14," the notice said, "All day of prayer and praise, 10 a.m. to 10 p.m., Central Hall, Westminster. Inauguration of Christ's Crusade by the farewelling of Mr. C. T. Studd and party for the Heart of Africa. Your prayers are earnestly invited for the outgoing party leaving Paddington on Monday, 24th, at 9.40 p.m. Confetti would be out of place, but a shower–bath of Hallelujahs is always in season."

Neither he nor Mrs. Studd had the remotest idea that this was his good–bye for ever to England, and almost his goodbye on earth to her, for in the next thirteen years they were only to meet for one bare fortnight, until they rejoined each other for ever before the Throne.

CHAPTER XVII

C. T. AMONGST THE NATIVES

THE party travelled by the West Coast to the mouth of the Congo River, 700 miles up by river steamer, and then another 300 miles through the forest by foot. The arrival at Nala was an amazing experience to C. T. Two years before he had left behind him just an unoccupied concession, a few deserted houses amidst a forest of palm trees.

"We had a wonderful reception at Nala [he wrote]. It was a vast, delighted crowd. For two years they had waited. Hope deferred had made their hearts sick at times, and led some to say I would never return. But when hope deferred becomes hope realized, the heart gets wonderfully robust. The folks, natives and native Christians, came out a long way to meet us. Dear old Sambo (the first convert at Nala) had come a day's march to welcome me. It was like a

Lord Mayor's Show. Four men carried a big native wooden drum on their heads with a little darkie on top beating it for all he was worth. Then there were bugles and throats blending wonderfully, and handshakings with the 'Nala touch' about them, which must now be the Crusader handshake. You first shake hands in ordinary fashion, but before you have fully unclasped, the other chap circles your thumb with his hand. It's quite amusing, especially when each party goes for the other chap's thumb, reminding one of the two snakes which swallowed each other's tails. So we marched straight to the house they had prepared for me, and there–we on the steps and they in the arena–the whole gave praise *fortissimo* to God in the Doxology. Then came the luxury of becoming a 'Knight of the Bath' once again.

"I was much struck with the quietness of the natives at worship ; their reverence was in inverse proportion to the comfort of their seats, which were benches composed, not of planks, but of three horizontal broomsticks about one inch apart! After sitting on one, I felt like Mr. Jacobs' night–watchman who sat for an hour on a wooden case, and then, on rising, turned round and, pointing to the box, said; 'Ah, I thought there was a nail there all the time!' There were some 60 Christians at Nala–not all of the same calibre, any more than are those who compose the congregations at home. Some I found, and still find, to be really fine fellows ; not two alike. But as I thought of three years ago, when Alfred and I had come here alone, it was indeed marvellous in my eyes." Then came a flying visit to Niangara, and the first white wedding in the heart of Africa. Four years had Alfred Buxton remained at his post of duty in spite of urgent calls to come home and claim his bride.

"The Commissioner was unable to come here to marry Alfred

and Edith [writes C. T. Studd], so we had to go up to Niangara, five days off. I shall never forget, as we crossed the bridge of the Nala river close by, the power with which the words came to me, 'With my staff I passed over this Jordan ; and now I am become two bands.' For were there not four of us going to Niangara, with a lot of Christian natives, and leaving behind ten other missionaries with the rest of the Christians?

"The Wedding Day was a full one. We went up the river in two canoes to our mission premises early in the morning for the English and Bangala service in the chapel there. Chapel? It was the first house we had possessed in Africa, which we had called 'Buckingham Palace,' and cost us no less than £6. We had breakfast beneath the same palm trees which had sheltered our tents when we first got the concession, and started to build. It was a day of remembrances indeed. There it was that I had received the mail alone that told me we had lost our two great champions–the late Lord Radstock and Mr. Martin Sutton–and God had at once given faith to believe and go ahead as though nothing really mattered but the backing of God. The day before we had strolled to the place in Niangara where for weeks we had lived in our tents, unable to find a suitable place in which to begin our labours. And was it not there that all of a sudden word came that the Chief had changed his mind and would let us have the haven where we would be? There it was that we gave him tea, and I left Alfred to sugar it well for him, while I went to Count de Grunne to tell him the good news, and found he was no less rejoiced than ourselves ; and there we slept the same night with such joyful hearts, for the thing had been settled quickly. There too I had slept with the snake and been delivered. One true word, at least ; the devil has said, 'Doth

Job serve God for nought?' Certainly not; neither Job nor his successors can do that.

"The service was sweet, and not over long. My ordination–that of D. L. Moody and Dr. Torrey–was the authority for the performance of the religious ceremony. The chapel was full, and the bride and bridegroom were as handsome and pretty as if it had been a St. George's, Hanover Square, affair. Then followed the native feast and congratulations, which occupied the time till our return in the canoes. It became a rush to get through in time for the legal service, which was attended by all the Belgian Officials in their full dress uniforms, medals and Orders. The Commissioner stood beside the Chef de District, who, as he read the preamble, shook with becoming nervousness. For was it not the first white wedding ever performed in the Heart of Africa? Twenty minutes sufficed for the ceremony, and then all came to tea, coffee, wedding cake, and the funniest French ever heard at the Chateau. The last thing was dinner with the Commissioner, a long affair.

"The bride and bridegroom, in spite of any nervous anxiety, behaved quite nicely, and were not unduly depressed, which enhanced the lofty ideas of the Commissioner and the Judge concerning British pluck! After the wedding, we had a photo taken of the bride and groom. It turned out to be what is called 'a speaking one!' Alfred was clearly saying, ' I've been and gone and done it, and feel I am still resigned' ; while Edith was saying, 'The future is all unknown, but I'm resolved to keep believing.'"

With what joy C. T. now settled to the work, making Nala his headquarters, and scattering his staff of missionaries to occupy Niangara, Poko and Bambili, the other three strategic centres of the Welle Province, and thus manning the four corners of a very rough square of territory about half the size of England, and containing some ten tribes.

"April, 1917. The work here is a marvel [he wrote], quite beyond my conception, the finger of God is writ all over it. We arrived here two strangers three and a half years ago, the natives sunk in sin unprintable, the medium of communication to be learned, yet there are now just upon 100 baptized converts. Many Chiefs are beginning to build schools and other houses at their centres, that we may go and instruct them and their people. Everywhere we have an open door for ourselves and our native Christians.

"81 have just been baptized. We had baptismal meetings for many days beforehand ; some especially those when the candidates gave their testimonies were remarkably interesting and lurid to a degree. I hear that some folk desire to be let into the dark side of missionary operations ; such should come out and hear the testimonies of the converts. I think there were hardly two who did not confess to having committed adultery frequently ; witchcraft was also practically universal. Among these folks adultery and fornication, so far from being considered sins, are reckoned as matters of course. Can you faintly imagine the condition of things when public opinion is on the side of sin, and when such things have obtained for generation after generation for hundreds of years back? When selfcontrol has been unknown and unpractised for so many generations, the lives of the people become lower than the brute beasts. Now you can perhaps imagine what a conversion means! Verily, as Paul said, it is not a recreation, but a new creation. Think again that sin is the only pastime they have, and the only thing they seem to live for. If every conversion at home is a miracle, any conversion here is a thousand times greater miracle.

"The day previous to the baptisms all once again made their solemn confession of faith and vowed to forsake all sin and walk worthy of their Saviour. Here's the testimony of one Jabori, 'after he had risen from the dead.' You can imagine how we pricked up our ears at the idea, for there also sat the very Jabori, one of the baptismal candidates. When we questioned the matter, we found many others testified to it being a fact, and finally Jabori himself before all told us this story : 'I was a great warrior ; I used to be sent by the Belgians to take villages and chiefs which they wanted to be subdued. At one time I became very ill and lost all consciousness and died. My friends had dug my grave and were putting me into it, when I rose up and said I had seen God Himself, Who told me that before long the English would come and tell us all about the true God and the truth. I told this vision to many, who were struck, and because of this the people used to speak of God by the name of "English."' All this was confirmed by numbers then present. God, as in Matthew i., still works by giving dreams to these people.

"The baptismal pool lies close to the Rungu Road, the river running under a rough trestle bridge. A large crowd had gathered and occupied the bridge and one shore of the river, while the other shore was chiefly reserved for the candidates. In the first score were three Chiefs, two of whom had built chapels in their villages. You may be sure there was much joy in Nala on that day.

"But if the 81 baptisms' day was great, there was a greater one to come. The best wine came last. Last January some 15 or 20 members of the Native Church went out to preach voluntarily for three months 'in the regions around and beyond.' They were paid the princely sum of three francs a head for board, keep travelling expenses, and incidentals for the three months, and yet some on their return to Nala handed back a franc, and others half a franc, to the Church fund from which their salaries had been paid. But this time 50 odd desired to go and preach. It was a lesson in how to evangelize these regions. We white evangelists have five porters each to carry our necessities ; they carried each his own. Each man or woman carried a bed, but this consists solely of a grass mat; the bedding consists of a thin blanket, if he has one at all ; the only lunch basket he possesses is always out of sight and beneath his belt, from which hang a jungle knife and an enamel cup. A straw hat on his head of his own make, a loin–cloth, and you have the Heart of Africa native missionary complete.

"The last impromptu meeting was under the mango tree. Here's my final advice to them :

"1. If you don't desire to meet the Devil during the day, meet Jesus before dawn.

"2. If you don't want the Devil to hit you, hit him first, and hit him with all your might, so that he may be too crippled to hit back. 'Preach the Word' is the rod the Devil fears and hates.

"3. If you don't want to fall–walk, and walk straight and walk fast!

"4. Three of the Devil's dogs with which he hunts us are:

Swelled head.
Laziness.
Cupidity.

"After final Prayer and Committal, they rushed up asking, 'How long are we to stay out? I replied, 'If you are tired, return at the end of one month ; if not, return at the end of two ; if you can stick three months, very good!' 'Oh, no!' said one beaming face with a mouth like a bullfrog and the chuckle of a turkeygobbler, 'I shan't be back for a year.' Whilst another continued, 'You won't see me again for eighteen months.' And off they went singing:

" I love Jesus Christ, Jesus loves me ;
And nothing else in the world matters,
So abounding joy possesses me."
Hallelujah!

"On their return, after describing their journeys and hardships, which were evidenced in the tattered condition of the few garments they possessed, Sambo, the first convert at Nala, said, 'But there was nothing outside that could take away the joy inside.'"

"August, 1917. There are now some 50 more men who desire baptism. One of them is my woodcutter and waterdrawer, Bondo by name. He is a man of speech also, and prays peculiar prayers which need interpretation, and his speeches are pungent. Some time ago he thus mixed up his prayer : "Thank You, thank You, Heavenly Father, thank You very much, You have killed my father and my mother, very many thanks, You have also given me salvation and washed my sins away and changed my heart, thank You very, very much, Heavenly Father ; and now I want You to convert my wife, and, if I have one wife I want You to wash away her sins and change her heart, and if I have two wives I desire You to do the same for both, thank You very much, Heavenly Father, Amen.' Of course, what he said about his father and mother was only a way of expressing their decease, and that he found no fault with God about the matter.

"The other day, when he put down his name for baptism, he thus delivered himself to Alfred, who asked, 'But, Bondo, what about your two wives?' 'Oh, that's all right,' said he ; 'I must have salvation, and I really only want one wife, and I think it is better to go to heaven than to have two wives ; yes, I think it is much better to go to heaven than to have three wives, so please put my name down!!!' But the best of this little speech of Bondo's is the revelation of what the natives themselves consider to be our attitude towards polygamy."

"May 31, 1918. The closer you live to these natives, the better. Keep them out of your house and off your verandah, and you will have as bad a time as you give them, and as bad an opinion of them as they have of you. Be thick with them, make them your friends, and they will be the most loving and joyful folks on earth, and make the tears come into your eyes on many and various occasions.

"The other day I was far from fit, so kept my bed longer than usual. Some of our Christians from a neighbouring village came in for early service. Seeing me from afar on my verandah in bed, they at once changed their route, and came to me in deep concern, which was only partly allayed when I assured them the name of my complaint was mostly 'laziness.' There upon they sat down around my bed. Conversation having come to an end, I wondered how I could get rid of these too loving folks without giving offence, and so be enabled to dress. Suddenly, to my consternation, I found the whole six kneeling round my bed, one after another letting out his heart in prayer for me. When the six had prayed, and before I could have my innings, the leader had pronounced the benediction, and a funny one it was too ! But the humour of it cleared the lump from my throat and mopped my eyes, so fortunately, being extra unconventional, I took my innings after the benediction. And yet these were by no means any of our 'classy' Christians, but some of the 'weaker brethren.' They may be weak or fail in the possession of many talents; but I knew that they possessed the greatest of all among God's gifts, 'Love.' These six were rank, raw and vicious heathen only twelve months ago, yet here they were with loosened tongue able to pray unasked and impromptu, and without a book."

"October 10. The progress is simply wonderful ; people are coming to us from every quarter and from very long distances. We are having pretty nearly weekly baptisms. The converts are evangelizing far and near. Many Chiefs are imploring us to send them teachers and are even building chapels and houses for us.

"Four men came a 20 days' journey to Nala, and when asked why, said, 'All the world knows there is much knowledge of God at Nala.' "

One trek also he had grand times, not now spying out the land, but visiting the Chiefs and evangelizing the people.

He writes of his visit to Chief Aboramasi :

"Leaving late in the afternoon we could not make the usual stage, but camped at dusk in a small village–a sandy roadside hamlet with an open shed, which did me handsome for the night.

"Next day the porters went ahead early ; I followed later on my cycle. I came to a broad stream with flood on either side ; by some chance a young man was on the other bank. He came at my call and carried my cycle across and then returned for me. He took me on his back, went three paces into the water, then wobbled and fell forward, and I over his head! There was nothing for it but to let out a good guffaw and go one's way rejoicing like the Ethiopian after his baptism.

"Overtaking my porters after some time, I found them haggling with a man who had shot a large monkey. Monkey cutlets are excellent–for the blacks! After a lot of palaver I bought the monkey. I wanted the skin to mend my banjo drum and they sighed for the substance, but alas! I think they are both skin and carcase, for I never saw it again. Probably it went into the soup.

"We started again. The boxes were lifted, but from one came out a dark liquid! The man had turned the box upside down and my tin of Nala homemade treacle had failed to hold tight. On opening the box I found 'Pan Treacoleum'–papers, books, letters, documents, clothes all living in too much brotherly harmony. It was extremely hot ; we were on an open plain. I had to send for water and wash the treacle from each paper, and then put them to dry in the sun. Thus we wasted two good hours, and felt we had been fried alive in the process.

"We only got into Aboramasi's village at dark and all were pretty tired. We only thought of food and bed. But God had something better in store than bed in a hurry. I had some rice ; the Chief came and his people. We sang hymns, and then worshipped; we were in the open with a bright fire and moonlight. The Chief and people were so interested and apprecia tive that they sat talking of the things of God and themselves. We forgot our weariness in the joy of telling of Jesus, and finding Him appreciated, so that when at last all had returned to their homes, and I could have a quiet time in my blankets, the hour was half past one a.m., yet one felt as gay as a lark.

"The next day the Chief, and his brothers chief, and crowds

came and occupied my house all day, and one could not but remember those Jews spending the whole day with Paul, speaking the things of the Kingdom of God. We spoke and sang all day. We have now over 90 hymns, jolly fine stuff too, no mistake about it ; you do not have to think whether noun or verb is playing hide and seek with you, as one has so often to do in what they call fine poetry. Ours hits you flat in the face every time and makes good hot texts for preachers. A special favourite goes :

"The road to hell is broad
    The devil keep it well swept :
Very many people travel on it
    Because madness has seized them.

The road to heaven is difficult,
    There is a stream to cross,
But there is only one canoe to ferry you over,
    The name of the canoe is Jesus.

"Then there is another to a very taking tune. The words mean :

"God doesn't love Mr. Lazybones,
    The devil binds such :
Men of labour don't fear hardship.
    No, God doesn't love laziness.

God looks after men of Jesus,
    But the devil tempts them,
Men of faith walk behind their Saviour.

"And we have one to a popular Salvation Army tune, one verse of which the natives specially like, as it hits their sorrows here. This is the translations :

"There are no taxes to pay in heaven,
One can rest there gratuitously.
Of soldiers and judges and prisons and courts of law,
And cato'ninetails there is not one.

Chorus : Let us go, let us go to the village of God, The village of joy and love.

"We shout them along the march and everywhere and it is quite amusing to hear a chap with a sudden fit of working energy upon the roof of his house burst out with 'God doesn't like Mr. Lazy-bones.'

"We had all day services, and then a lantern service in the evening. I had to operate and also explain the pictures. Then I gave them a bit off my own bat, urging acceptance of Christ. I am a poor Bangala speaker, and so I said to Boemi, 'Now's your innings. They may not have understood my edition, so give them yours.' So B. began, 'Brothers all, I am going to say a few words in case you have not understood the words of Bwana (C.T.S.)' ; but from the Chief and people came a perfect storm of 'Wapi! Wapi!' which translated would mean as follows : 'Stuff and nonsense, we understand every word.' So you see the God of miracles is still alive and can even interpret my clumsy, unsatisfactory sentences to the people. Then up rose the Chief and spoke in his own lingo to the people, and they responded, and then came a moment which the wealth of heaven and earth cannot buy, for he said, 'I and my people, and my brother chief and his people, desire to tell you that we believe these things about God and Jesus and ourselves, and we all want to travel the same road as you–the road to heaven."

Meanwhile a new door had opened and been occupied, the door into the Ituri Province. When coming through to Nala from the Congo, Mr. Studd had been led to return by an unusual route. At one place a Chief visited him and offered him a plot of ground, if he would come and teach them. It turned out to be the lovely hill of Deti, from which a glorious view is obtained of the forest and grass land for miles around. This became the first station in the Ituri Province, and from it developed the great Ituri work, which, both in the numbers and readiness of the people to accept the Gospel, has altogether surpassed the work in the Welle Province. One of the earliest converts was the blind Ndubani, whose eyes had been put out by having red pepper rubbed into them, to prevent him becoming Chief. He had a dream in which he saw flames rising at the end of the road upon which he was walking, and heard a voice saying, "Wait for the white man with the book and he will tell you how to escape the flames." He has been a faithful witness ever since, tapping his way round the villages, led by his son, and preaching the Gospel. The great chief of that district, Abiengama, was a cannibal and had recently captured and eaten 14 native porters. But when his chief wife heard for the first time of the great, loving God, she exclaimed, "I always said there ought to be a God like that." The first missionaries to be sent there were Mr. and Mrs. Ellis. Mr. Studd visited them in June, 1918, and was amazed at what he saw :

"At Deti Hill I was enabled to stay for a week–end to see the work, and truly it is wonderful. The Worship Shed I found had been greatly enlarged, and Mrs. Ellis told me it would be packed out next day, which would be Sunday. Soon after dawn the folks began to arrive. Deti is situated on a high hill ; it is a good climb up, and so all the worshippers had to tackle the hill. We had early breakfast, then I went to my room for a little while, and soon after, when the drum had been beaten, I went to the–well, I suppose I must call it a church, though it is just a grass hut, grass roof and grass walls. I found the place simply packed with black shiny bodies, closer than peas in a pod. It seemed as if each black body touched four other bodies, like a lot of acidulated lemon drops that have been exposed to heat and run into each other. It was the work of some minutes to get into the middle of this medley of roast beef and take my stand at one end, jammed up against the grass wall. I could feel the heat of the seething mass of men, women, and children ; everybody shone with oil well rubbed in, and every face shone with an intensely eager gaze, like when a child expects the bird to fly out of the lens of the camera.

"Then the service began. It was in Kingwana, and so in an unknown tongue as far as I was concerned. The singing was remarkably good and accurate and went with a snap. You could hear the individual words, which to me is the test of good singing ; not merely emitting a pleasant humming sound or buzz. Then the Lord's Prayer, and another prayer and a passage of Scripture, all interspersed with hymns. Then came my turn. I had to give them a talk. There were several sub–chiefs of the great Chief Abiengama sit ting in front of me, my knees touching theirs as I stood, so rightly were we jammed together.

I began a bit nervously. I hate interpreter speaking ; but the sight of that eager, listening crowd soon produced the proper fever temperature, and one felt, When shall I see these folks again? And it became the experience of that framed verse I once saw in the Rev. Webb People's vestry, and so learned the secret of his fiercely earnest speaking :

"I'll preach as though I ne'er shall preach again,
And as a dying man to dying men!

"It seemed absolutely impossible to speak sentence by sentence, so I fired off now short and now long, and had to trust to the interpreter catching the sense and retailing it aright. As we warmed up, novel experiences arrived, for as Munganga finished, now one sub-chief and now another, who knew Bangala, would shout out or prompt Munganga concerning some point he had left out. Then a hymn, and Ellis spoke a few words, and the great service was over. Never could I forget that service, even though I wished to do so–the living, anxious look on the faces intent on catching every word! And then my mind wandered back to just one year ago, when Deti was only a hilltop bare of everything but the elephant grass and jungle undergrowth of Africa. There Alfred Buxton and Ellis and I had gone to inspect Abiengama's gift of the hilltop; and there we had drawn aside to sit on the grass or trunk of a tree, to thank God for His gift of the place in which to begin our work. Once again came the drumming of my heart with the message, 'This is the finger of God,' and 'What hath God wrought !' "

Three years were thus occupied, and then C.T. had to say good-bye to his "Timothy," Alfred Buxton. For six years they had worked together. Alfred had been to him "as a son with the father, he hath served with me in the Gospel." Has there ever been another example of a young man at the age of twenty penetrating into the heart of a savage country, left alone after two years, reducing the language to writing, and building up the first Church of Jesus Christ among an ignorant, semi–naked, and desperately–depraved people? C.T. had already written home of him after their early pioneer journeys together :

"To Alfred's nursing and care I certainly, under God, owe my life ; and truly no mother ever nursed her child more tenderly and efficiently than he nursed me. During close on two years we lived together in the closest possible intimacy, sharing the same hut, and nearly always the same tent or room. In trials many, in sickness and pain, in bereavements and the many malicious attacks of the evil one, unavoidable to those who attack the virgin fortresses of the devil, Alfred was ever to me a loyal son and heart companion. None but God can ever know the deep fellowship, joy and affection of our daily social and spiritual communion, for no words can describe it."

The public farewell was in Nala Church.

"A hurried breakfast [Alfred wrote] and all were gathered in the Church. I spoke of the work before me, and how inefficient I was for it, and reminded them of C.T.'s word the day before, of how the Spirit of Elijah rested on Elisha. And I asked C.T. to lay his hands on me. As I sat down, C.T. got up and whispered, 'You must do what I tell you, then,' and setting his chair he bade me mount it. I did so, and then, as he spoke, I realised what he intended to do. This man, twice my age, a missionary more than five times as long as I, who had done ten thousand times more for God than I, this man refused to lay his hands on my head, and chose instead, my feet. I could only submit, but when his prayer was done, I said, as soon as I was off the chair, 'Bwana has played a trick on me to-day, but it was a trick of love'; and then it was hard to go on, but I could at last, and said, 'But I want you to remember the lesson he has taught you to-day. Jesus once washed Peter's feet ; I did not object, like Peter, because I wanted Bwana to lay his hands on me ; but I want you to remember that though Jesus washed His disciples' feet, yet He was still their Lord and Leader, and so it is with Bwana and me to-day.'

"Half an hour later we were on the road. The whole of Nala came to see us off, and what with good byes and handshakes every few yards, it took us three hours to do what would usually take one."

With Alfred had gone his wife and four others needing a furlough, and baby Susan, the first white baby born in the Heart of Africa. She had been dedicated to God in the Nala Church together with a number of black babies, the children of Christian parents. This had left the staff on the Field seriously depleted. Parties had not been able to come out during the past eighteen months because of the stress of the War in 1917 and 1918, and a few had left the work. Then followed a period of great testing, testing through shortage of workers, through illhealth, but above all, through the heartbreak of backsliding. Some o f the leading Christians fell into sin, and C.T. became increasingly conscious of the need of a deeper work of God in the hearts of the people. Later experiences at Ibambi increased and confirmed this conviction and drove them to seek God's face more earnestly than ever for an outpouring of the Spirit .The sequel is seen in a later chapter. The little band of six held on grimly with their backs to the wall, one at Deti, one at

Poko, one evangelizing in the Ituri, and Bwana (G.T.) with two ladies, Nurse Arnall (now Mrs. Staniford) and Miss Bromberger at Nala.

"I have been having an awful time [he wrote to his mother in May, 1920], with terrible irritation of the arms and legs, and many bad ulcers on the feet and ankles ; the irritation is sometimes maddening ; but really we ought to have something, considering how little we have suffered.

"I think disappointments are the greatest sufferings. As Paul said, 'We live if ye (our converts) stand fast in the Lord,' and the disappointment of a backsliding Christian seems to rob one of all vitality.

"[And to his wife.] The heart is torn out of one by the doings of some of these folk, and , alas, by the old hands ; deceit , lying and uncleanness have been frequent, so that one has often about lost heart and cried out, 'Who's next?' However, there are some faithful ones, so one rejoices in them, as also in God." Among the encouragements of these days were the early morning Prayer Meeting which he started :

"You should hear these folks at the 5 a.m. daily Prayer meeting in the Cutty-Cutty (centre part of the house). We have this before sunrise. The meeting is suppose to be at 5.30, but they troop down at 5 a.m., and begin singing and praying ; and oh, the prayers they pray! No humdrum affair, these, but redhot shots from their very hearts.

"One night I was very late at work ; it was 2 a.m., and it was not worth while going to bed for an hour and a half, so I thought of lying down as I was. I was just blowing out the candle, when sure enough, there was a black form on a chair near by. As I looked, he broke out with his excuse for coming. 'I could not sleep, I must receive the Holy Ghost! Will you not pray for me?' Was there ever such an electric shock galvanizing into new life a dog-tired puddinghead, such as I then was? Never! This was real medicine. We prayed, and then I got him a long chair and put him in it by the fire while I lay down on the bed.

"I often think it is just the prayers of these people (and of course of you all at home) that keep me alive. Whatever else escape their memory, in their prayers they never forget to pray as follows : 'And there's Bwana, Lord, he is a very aged man (60), his strength is no use, give him yours, Lord, and the Holy Ghost as well.' Did I tell you of the man who thus prayed for me? 'Oh, Lord, you have been indeed good to have caused Bwana to live ten years on earth, now cause him to live two years more.' "

Relief came in the Spring of 1920. Mrs. Studd and the Committee at home had so felt the necessity of sending reinforcements, that they got to prayer, andb although they knew of none ready at the time, sent a cable by faith in the summer of 1919, "Reinforcements leaving *this year*." God answered, and seven days before the year closed, the first party sailed. It included his youngest daughter Pauline and her husband. They were followed within a month or two by two further parties, all of men now released from the War ; and from that time onwards there was a steady stream of recruits, so that within three years the workers increased from six to nearly forty.

Meanwhile, the regions beyond were urgently calling. C.T. had never forgotten those crowds and crowds of people who had mobbed them as they cycled along on their first journey through the Ituri forest ; and now he was receiving reports from both native evangelists and missionaries of thousands clamouring to be taught. The return of Alfred Buxton in 1921 to take on the work at Nala made it possible for him to go further afield. So with all the joy of the pioneer evangelist, he turned his face toward the white harvest-field of the Ituri Province.

CHAPTER XVIII

FORWARD EVER, BACKWARD NEVER !

IN the Ituri forest, four days south of Nala, lived a big chief, named Ibambi. It was evident that his village was the centre of a great population. To reach it one walked for hours along a path where the virgin forest had been cleared back for a hundred yards on each side. Lofty palm trees, with their beautiful crowns, grew everywhere in disordered profusion, and all along the pathway beneath their shade, nestling amongst banana trees with their huge green leaves and great bunches of fruit, were myriads of the neatest of bamboo huts. These little dwellings were real works of art, with their bamboo walls tied together with fiber from the palm tree, leaf roof and leaf door.

There seemed to be simply no end to the people, their almost naked bodies shining with palm oil, their wiry black hair plaited with extreme care into all sorts of fantastic shapes, their curious longshaped heads. Their sole clothing was a piece of very coarse bark–cloth wrapped around their thighs, the men wore considerably more than the women, and on the heads of the men and boys were straw hats, often plaited with beautiful colour designs and kept in place by long ivory hatpins.

To the casual observer they seem both happy and healthy, as they shout out the news from one hut to another that a white man is passing, and men and women and boys and girls all pour out, spear and bow in hand, with the abandon of children, laughing FORWARD EVER, BACKWARD NEVER! and running and singing as they flock round his cycle.

But experience tells a very different story. Stop in a village with a few medicines and see them come in, children with sores from head to foot, men and women with gaping ulcers on their legs, the fingerless and toeless leper, babies with their little soft heads squeezed out of shape by the cord bound tightly around, according to the universal custom which demands that the shape of their heads must be, not round, but long and narrow. Talk to them and watch their faces, the furrows on the foreheads of the old men, not merely of old age but of fear and darkness and devilry ; gross sensuality and cruelty on nearly every face. Get inside their lives as best a white man may, and learn of the utter debauchery, so that neither lad nor girl is pure, "who being past feeling have given themselves over unto lasciviousness, to work all uncleanness with greediness"; the stranglehold of the witchcraft upon them, a mixture of fear and murder and beastliness, fear of evil spirits all around them, murder because of their never–ending attempts to do away with neigh–bours or relatives by working witchcraft on them, and beastliness because of the unnameable rituals of these secret societies ; marriage almost always a purely business contract between father and suitor, bringing the father more "wealth" to buy himself another wife, and the husband a drudge and mother for his children. See their hopeless ignorance ; they have never once heard of a God who loves and cares, they have no conception of holiness or heaven, they have never seen a book. And see yet one step further. See as God sees : see hearts that can be washed whit e as snow and their very desires changed : see souls that can receive eternal life : see bodies that can be possessed by the Spirit of Christ and all their powers used to show Him forth. And then we see the Divine Urge that drove C.T. on to capture this good land for Christ.

In 1992 he moved his headquarters to Ibambi. By now he was famous for many miles around, the gaunt figure with the thick beard, aquiline nose, burning words and yet merry laugh. He was as much the apostle to that region as Paul to Asia Minor, and they called him just "Bwana Mukubwa" (Great White Chief). Many are called "Bwana" (White Chief), but none except he was ever "Bwana Mukubwa." The missionaries used to call him "Bwana" for short, and we shall often use that name.

Ibambi became the headquarters of the Mission. He found the numbers and eagerness of the people to hear no whit exaggerated, and it can be imagined with what joy he threw himself into instructing them.

"Here was a chance to set the whole of the Heart of Africa ablaze with the knowledge of the Cross and love of God. For such an end all should once again go joyfully into the meltingpot, there could be no talk of returning home."

First to Ibambi itself they came by the hundred to be taught and baptized."

"We were besieged by people coming for baptism. Almost every day one could hear the hymns of people coming from various directions."

Then he began to go out into the forest area around. He visited Imbai's, five hours from Ibambi, where the head man of the village had asked for a teacher :

"The sound of abundance of rain ! [he wrote]. What music it is to tired hearts and heavy ears to hear the sound of hymnsinging ever coming closer and closer, and then to see a band of men and women, boys and girls, who have marched one or two or eight or ten hours to hear the words of God. I found some 1,500 blacks, all packed tight as sardines, squatting on the ground in the sweltering mid–day African sun. No church nor shed was theirs. They are singing hymns to God with hearts and tongues and voices–a great untrained and unpaid choir, making better melody to God and to us than a choir of a thousand Carusos. You watch their eager faces as they squat there drinking in every word of the preacher. They are greedy for the Gospel. A two hours' meeting doesn't trouble them, unless it be that they consider it scant measure. They were then sent for a rest for an hour ; then they turned up bright and greedy as ever for their second innings. "Under our supervision they built themselves a House of God to seat 1,250 people. It measured as much as a cricket pitch each way. They did it in record time. They had far to travel to get the grass for the roof, and were evidently tired. Said a Crusader, 'Would it not be well to send them home for a week, and then let them return to finish?' 'Certainly ! Tell them they have done well, and in two weeks' time they can come to finish the work.' Their reply was, 'What? Do you think we are going to undertake to build a House of God, and are going home with it unfinished?' "

At Adzangwe's, three hours away, it was the same. "Five or six hundred go to his village of a Sunday to worship [wrote C.T.]. We had gone on a weekday and a crowd await ed us, and eagerly they listened as we taught them of sin and righteousness and judgment to come, and Jesus. Adzangwe had heard of the building of the 'Cricketpitch Church' and wanted one for his people, that they might worship God in spite of storms and sun. And this is what he said to my fellow–Crusader, 'Bwana is now tired and he is ill with his exertion over building the House of God at Imbai's. He must go and rest now, but afterwards will he come and teach us to build a House of God here?' What answer could there be? 'No ! Bwana is going home to England where all have heard of Christ and where there are churches and chapels and missionrooms galore, and he is going to leave your people to rush headlong into hell?' Could it be?

"One of my fellow–Crusaders held up a coin to explain the gift of Salvation and said, 'The first who comes shall have it.' The reply he received gave him the shock of his life, 'But, Sir, we have not come for money, but to hear the words of God.'

"Another had spoken long, and, as he closed, he apologized. The voice of an old man came from the midst of the black throng, 'Don't stop, Sir, don't stop! Some of us are very old and have never heard these words before, and have but little time to hear in future."

Half a dozen other places were the same, Badua's, Bakondangama's, Adzoka's, etc. Bwana had indeed found his "Eldorado." Much pressure was brought to bear on him to persuade him to go home, but he had begun to reap a ripened harvest and he would not

"How could I spend the best years of my life in living for the honours of this world, when thousands of souls are perishing every day?" -- C.T.S.

GENTLEMEN OF ENGLAND, 1884
Back - A.P. Lucas Lord Harris, C.T. Studd
Centre - W.E. Roller, A.W. Ridley, Dr. W.G. Grace, E. J. Diver, A.G. Steel
Front - F.T. Welman, W.W. Read, S. Christopherson

A FEW OF C.T.'S FRIENDS IN THE HEART OF AFRICA, 1926

be moved, neither now nor later. He always gave the same answer, that God had told him to come out when every voice was raised against him, and that only God could tell him when to go home. To one who reproved him for not going home, he wrote :

"Had I cared for the comments of people, I should never have been a Missionary and there would never have been an H.A.M. As Micaiah said, 'The Word that God gives me to speak I shall speak,' so also the work that God gives me to do I shall strive to accomplish or die in the attempt.

"Seeing that some 40 years ago at God's command I left mother, brethren, friends, fortune and all that is usually though to make life worth living, and have so continued ever since, have been called fool and fanatic again and again, yet lived to prove that the worldly counsellors were the fools, I don't think I should much enjoy ending up in being frightened out of doing my duty by hearkening to the comments of men. 'Cursed is he that trusteth in man' does not make a very good pillow for a dying man, but there is much comfort in the other one, 'Blessed is he that trusteth in the Lord.' "And do you think that I can consent to turn a deaf ear to the cries of these people clamouring for the Gospel and craving for teachers? If I can't send them teachers because there are no teachers to send, yet at least I can stop one yawning gap myself. If I am not so efficient as youngsters, yet at least I may be more efficient than an absentee, a nobody. And if others have failed to hear and respond to these awful pleadings of sinful men going to hell, yet desiring to know the way to heaven, at least my presence can assure them that there are still some who to save them will count life and all they hold dear as of no account in comparison.

"God knows all about my health and need of a rest and need

of many things regarded as absolutely necessary in order to live in these regions. I gladly laugh at being without them, and rejoice in a living death with a marvellous joy, in order to fill the place that others have left unoccupied whatever their reasons for so doing."

By 1923 there were forty Crusaders on the Field, so that, few though they were for this vast area, at least some further strategic points could be occupied in the Ituri Province ; and soon stations had been opened at Deti, Ibambi, Wamba, Botongwe, and even Bomili and Panga in the far south, besides, of course, the four stations in the Welle Province. Yes, it had been well worth while to have obeyed God's call in 1913.

CHAPTER XIX

THE GOD OF WONDERS

THE day after C.T. left for Africa in 1916, his wife launched out in faith. We do not know whether she had in mind the letter in which he had urged her to trust Jesus for the body, as in China ; but she did it. She got off her invalid's couch by faith, never to return to it again.

"Mother 's resurrection is the greatest miracle I know of [wrote C.T. to Alfred Buxton]. I cannot say what joy it gives me. She is now like what she used to be in China. I have never seen anyone to compare with her–man or woman–when she gets going ; she has such energy and vision and faith that she can capture anybody.

"Surely God was waiting for some simple act of faith [he wrote later], to send down His cyclone of blessing. That cyclone hit my wife the very day after I left, and she was never the same woman again. There was no invalid about her ; she became a cyclone, became the Mission's chief deputation secretary, as well as a great many other things besides. God took her to U.S.A., Canada, Australia, New Zealand, Tasmania, and South Africa. She lived the life of a whirlwind ; she had no other thought than the salvation of souls and the care of her children."

There was not a finer missionary speaker in the country. She spoke as though she herself lived through all her husband's experiences in Africa. Her descriptions were no mere word-pictures ; there was blood and fire in them, not the outflow of a clever imagination, but of a bleeding heart, daily sacrificing for Christ and the heathen the one who was dearer than life to her. None knew the daily cross she carried ; the distance that separated them ; the longing for his sympathy and advice in the work ; the anxiety as each mail arrived telling of his labours and weakness and fevers ; the inability to be with him and to succour him. The founders of the H.A.M. indeed went Christ's way, "Except a corn of wheat fall into the ground and die, it abideth alone ; but if it die, it bringeth forth much fruit." Career and fortune had early gone on the altar, now health and home and family life went also. Indeed, C.T. once said, "I have searched into my life and do not know of anything else left that I can sacrifice to the Lord Jesus."

Many who heard her Annual Meeting addresses will never forget them, and many heard the call as she spoke. There was the address when she appealed for "Ten W.E.C.H.A.M. Fearnots," with these characteristics, they must be :

Noroadmen!
Takeyourlifeinyourhandsmen!
Flameoffiremen!

Brainerdmen!

Another address was headed, "Five packed minutes o n a Crazy Mission," in which she quo ted the following :

"Just listen to this extract from a letter from a friend : 'We read your Magazine with interest. You are, humanly speaking, one of the craziest Missionary Societies that ever existed ; but if sanit y means Modernism and no souls, may God grant you may never be same!' And so say all of us!"

God had already given Mr. and Mrs. Studd No. 17, Highland Road, Upper Norwood, as the Headquarters of the Mission. C.T. had been distinctly guided to buy it in 1913, when there was no thought of a Mission at all, and equally wonderfully guided in the purchase of the furniture :

"I saw a house that looked the very thing, and at a wonderfully reasonable price. That house was one of the impressions of my life. Little did I dream that it was to be the headquarters of a new mission, and that my wife was to become its presiding genius ; but I felt I had to have it. In a short time God provided for it and gave it to me. Then we went to see about the furniture. We went to a good many cheap places, but not even the cheapest suited our purse, so we made very few purchases. One day I was going down Westbourne Grove, and saw some secondhand furniture standing outside a shop. No one was inside ; the back door was open and led into a large room where there was a great deal of furniture and a sprinkling of people ; so I went in, found there was an auction on, and saw things being knocked down at the most ridiculous prices. Before leaving, I had invested in a library chair upholstered in morocco, in walnut wood, for which I paid the fancy price of fifteen shillings. The next week I went down there again and was successful in obtaining more furniture at similar fancy prices. Then I heard there was going to be a big auction sale by the same firm in another place. Of course we had decided to carpet our house from top to bottom with linoleum, as good for wear and not subject to tear. We had bought a few things, when some carpets came up for sale. These did not interest me at all, and I had turned aside to examine the catalogue. A poke in the ribs brought me to attention.

'Charlie, do you see what those carpets are going for?' 'No,' I replied, 'I am not interested in them ; "lino" is the thing for me.' 'But,' she said, 'look here. A carpet has just gone at a far cheaper price than we could purchase any linoleum.' I am afraid I doubted until I saw the next carpet go up, and that I bought, and several others, for indeed it was a fact. But of course the carpet had to be bordered with linoleum. One of the last things at the auction was a lot of six rolls of linoleum, all of the same pattern and evidently out of the same house. We bought the whole six for thirty shillings, and with those six we 'lino'd' the whole house.

"Another day I went to an auction held in a private house. One of the last things put up were the electric light fitting. I had not looked at them, I did not know how many there were–there was not time to go into the other rooms and see–and until then I had no thought of having electric light in the house, for electricity had not come to our road ; but all those fittings went for thirty-two shillings and I was the purchaser, and that thirtytwo bobs' worth are the electric light fitting of No. 17. Chairs, tables, beds, sideboards, and even pictures all came from the same source, and all at the same fancy prices. This is the way our Father supplied the furniture. Now for the sequel. I had to leave London. I asked my mother as a great favour if she would allow her butler to go to the auction room and buy a bookcase for me. At the end of the month I returned. As soon as the butler opened the door, I said, 'Well, Ryall, how many bookcases?' A very sad look came across his face as he replied, 'Mr. Charles, not one. I'll tell you about it. You must carry about with you that fairy godmother of whom we sometimes hear, for I went down to the auction room each week. There were bookcases which would have suited your house, but not your purse ; and all the time I was there I never saw anything go for a bargain price such as you have been accustomed to give.' That is the true story of the magnificence of the furniture of No. 17."

For a time No. 17 made a splendid Mission house and offices, but as t he work expanded, guests, candidates, returned missionaries, office workers, and masses of literature became too much of a good thing. Then in 1921, faith leapt over the wall–this time the faith of the cook as well as of Mrs. Studd–and a splendid set of offices, standing in their own garden, consisting of seven rooms and a large loft, which could seat fifty people prayer meetings, were added to Head quarters, at an annual rent which is no more than the rent of one room in the City. Mrs. C.T. tells the story herself :

"In the early days of our work, C.T.'s pen was very prolific, and in rolled booklet after booklet from Africa. It was in the days when I was a confirmed invalid, and spent half of every day in bed. Enter a very irate cook. 'Please, ma'am, 10,000 booklets from the printers, and where shall I put them?' 'Oh ! can't you place the packets along the walls in the basement passages?' Cook : 'How am I to wash the floors with a lot of books along the walls? How are we all to keep well with a lot of dusty packets?' 'Well, put them in here along the walls in my bedroom.' No, that would not do. 'Well, I don't Know–put them on the roof !' Exit a more irate cook.

"This happened more than once. Then another day she came and said, 'Please, ma'am, you get so many answers to prayers, I wish you would pray and ask the Lord to empty that garage next door and put all this literature in there.' 'A sheer impossibility,' I replied. 'That garage belongs to the biggest doctor in the place–he has three cars there, and horses. But look here', said I, 'there's something for you to do, you go and pray the chauffeur out !'

"The spring came and one day again entered cook : 'Please, ma'am, will you get up and come to the window and see, that chauffeur is not digging his garden this spring.' 'Well, what of that?' 'Well, it means he's going.' 'Oh, yes!' I replied, 'you think so?' (rather ironically). 'Sure of it,' replied the cook. 'Well, we'll wait and see.' 'Sure enough, before the autumn the chauffeur was called up as a mechanic in the Air Force. The doctor's big cars had to go and the garage was empty ! 'Now what are you going to do? 'said the cook. It was War time. 'Oh, well, I can't take on any more financial responsibility than I have already got.' I shelved the matter and my conscience so smote me over it that finally when the board 'To be Let' was taken down, I thought, 'Oh, I am so glad that place is taken.' Taken ! Who do you think came and took it? A cracked old lady came and took it for a Dogs' and Cats' Home!
"Oh, the irony of God ! I hadn't the faith to trust God for another ?100 a year. The Cat's and Dogs' Home became a menance not only to my own home, but to the whole distinct, and to make a long story short–Fish bones! Meat bones ! Dogs' bones ! Cats' bones ! became so intolerable in the hot summer weather, that I had

to complain to the Medical Officer of Health on my own and my neighbours' accounts, and out went the cracked lady and up went the board 'To Let!'

"Garage empty again! Still I hedged. Again the board came down, once more to my intense relief ! I went away to Scotland, but my Secretary wrote me there : 'The garage board "To Let" is up again. What will you do?' Finally, I wrote to Mr. Barclay, 'I hear that the garage is "To Let" again, I think we must go forward and rent it ; I dare not say "No" again.' After some hitches the garage became ours, and now we have 17 and 19, Highland Road, and I hear people say that they don't want to live in our road lest we should want their house and pray them out ![4] So that was how I was compelled to jump over a wall, and 'He hath triumphed gloriously,' after all, in spite of me!"

The coming of Mr. Gilbert Barclay, Dorothy's husband, into the work in 1919 for eight years as Home Overseer was not only a tremendous help to Mrs. Studd, but also the beginning of a new era in the Crusade.

Although the original vision given to C.T. had been "To every unevangelized land," attention had so far been entirely concentrated on the first advance–to the Heart of Africa. Gilbert Barclay came into the work on the condition that the Crusade should now be given a worldwide title, and that other lands should be entered forthwith, as God directed and enabled. The title "Worldwide Evangelization Crusade" was adopted, each separate Field having its own subtitle, such as "The Heart of Africa Mission." By

4 Recently the house on the opposite side of the road, No. 34, has been bought by a friend of the Mission's, Miss. L. Gristwood, who is going to live there herself and use her house as an additional W.E.C., Mission House.

magazine and deputation work attention was drawn to the needs of other lands, with the result that in 1922 three young men set forth on the second advance of the Crusade–The Heart of Amazonia Mission. They went to the Red Indians of the Amazon, one of the most difficult missionary problems of the world, scattered remnants of a once great racenaked, often ferocious, buried in the vast Amazon forests like needles in a haystack–yet each with a soul beyond price, bought with Christ's Blood. The searching out of some of these tribes and the starting of a Gospel work among them has been an epic of Christian heroism. To reach the Guajajara tribe cost Fenton Hall his life, but three young Australians immediately filled the gap, and to–day, ten years after, converted Guajajaras, with portions of the Scriptures in their own tongue, are now scattered amongst the villages evangelizing their own people.

Kenneth Grubb and Harold Morris were tortured and almost starved to death in their attempt to start work among the Parentintin tribe, 1,200 miles up the Amazon. But they persisted, and missionaries lived among them some four years, until the tribe so dwindled in numbers that the workers had to move elsewhere.

Gradually the Amazonian work became established, and at the time of C.T.'s death there was a staff of some sixteen missionaries with a Headquarters and Stations in three tribes. To–day the work, although now independent, is going ahead both with Indian and Brazilian evangelization.

The third advance was to Central Asia. Only two men went, Jock Purves and Rex Bavington, beyond the northern frontiers of India. Here they worked in close cooperation with the Central Asian Mission, founded by Colonel G. Wingate, crossing a 16,000 feet pass of the Himalaya Range into the lonely land of Little Tibet, where no Eurpoean, except missionaries, has ever lived. They lived native fashion amongst the Baltis–a poor, halfstarved, neglected and dirty people, scraping a livelihood from the barren slopes of the mountain ranges. There have been two converts among these fanatical Moslems, and many more who are inquirers. Recently the CentralAsian Mission has amalgamated with the W.E.C., so now the work goes forward with a present staff of nine missionaries in four stations, and with vast unevangelized areas before them, which must be prayed open before they can be entered, owing to the opposition of Governments, and Moslem fanaticism.

A fourth and yet a fifth advance were made to Arabia and West Africa, respectively. Both failed at first attempt, the pioneer to Arabia returning home and the one to West Africa–Alfred Hawley–dying within a year. But now the Heart of Arabia Mission is again established, Jack Wilson having learnt Arabic, bought a house in a desert city of Northern Arabia, from which he goes forth on camel back and in Arab dress to evangelize the Bedouin. Twice already his life has been threatened, but the Lord has given him one wonderful open door a Bedouin tribe, who have Christian traditions dating back from preMoslem times, and who, though no longer carrying on any form of Christian worship, are eager that he should come and teach them. Another Crusader is now learning Arabic and about to join him.

West Africa is being again attempted by a couple on their way to open work in Spanish Guinea ; and yet another field has been entered in South America, the Republic of Colombia. Pat Symes is already out there, selecting the best area in which to start work, and three others will have joined him by the time that this book is in print.

No appeal was ever made for funds, no collections taken at meetings, nor plates at the door, nor any other means used to stimulate giving, such as sales of work, bazaars, etc. The work was started and is carreid on in absolute trust in the faithfulness of God, who promised, "Seek ye first the kingdom of God, and His righteousness; and all these things shall be added unto you. " The Home Committee in no sense hold themselves responsible for the support of the missionaries ; they are merely channels of supply ; they are not even concerned whether the monthly sums forwarded to the Field are much or little ; they carry no burden about it, for that is a matter solely between Master and servant, Father and children. There are no fixed salaries or allowances on any Field ; each month just such sums as are sent in for the various Fields are forwarded to them for equal division amongst the workers. No grumbles are heard in any of the "camps," for as Mr. Harrison, who has taken Mr. Studd's place in the Heart of Africa, writes :

"For myself, I am gloriously free from anything in the way of a 'load' concerning money matters, and whether it be for things personal, or things for the running of a station, or things for the work in general, I myself will stand to this testimony :

> Oh, this life of faith is certainly worth living,
> And there's not a moment dull throughout the year,
> For the cruse of oil is never, never failing,
> And the meal tub's always got a handful more.
>
> Hallelujah!"

By God's good hand upon us throughout the twenty years of the Crusade's existence, it has never been in debt. Up to the time of Mr. Studd's death, God had sent no less a sum than £146,746 Is. 3*d*. Did we not say earlier on that we should see how faithful God is to those who leave all and follow Him? In those twenty years alone God gave back to C.T. nearly five times the amount he gave to God in China. Neither C.T. nor Mrs. Studd ever touched a penny of Mission money for personal use, as C.T. wrote to her in 1918 :

"Don't take a penny from H.A.M. We stand and will stand upon God, and though He slay me, yet will I trust in Him. He is only proving our love and trust in Him ; so welcome penury. Don't get rid of K. or J. or anyone, we will all trust God together and *we shall swim* ; yes, we shall not sink, He will not let us, and this very trust will be our testimony that we are of Him. Who ever trusted in Him and was confounded? No, not one penny will we take but what He sends, and be sure He will send."

One of the ways God provided was by moving two hidden friends, whom it is doubtful whether C.T. himself ever met, to send him again and again gifts of £ 500 and £1,000 for his personal use on the Field.

The "personal use" consisted of the money being stored in a large steel trunk in his bamboo hut, and then distributed to further the work and help his fellow workers. Is God any man's debtor?

CHAPTER XX

WHEN THE HOLY GHOST CAME

YEARS ago in China, BoothTucker had written to C.T., "Remember that mere soul–saving is comparatively easy work, and is not nearly so important as that of manufacturing the saved ones into Saints, Soldiers and Saviours." This challenge now faced C.T. in the Heart of Africa. While he had been at Nala, there had been first a period of much apparent response and many baptisms, then many disappointments, evidence of sin, slothfulness and self–seeking amongst even leading Christians and evangelists, and an obvious need of an outpouring of the Holy Ghost. He was now face to face with the same thing in the Ituri Province. From the beginning of his missionary career he had never been satisfied with a shallow work. He had had early shocks in China, when he had visited stations with a big reputation, and found on closer inspection but little evidence of a deep work of God. Now it confronted him in his own work, and he set himself to give God and the people no rest until the Holy Ghost should come upon them. From both Scripture and experience he denounced a faith that produced no works as a spurious faith.

"Christ came to save us by His Blood and by His Spirit, Blood to wash away our past sins, Spirit to change our hearts and empower us to live right. He came not to save us *in* our sins but *from* them. He came to save sinners, and to make them righteous. Christ never died to enable a man to sin with im punity ; 'My sheep follow Me,' and those who follow Christ walk like Christ, and that was not in sin. John said, 'Whosoever doeth not righteousness is not of God' and 'He that doeth sin is of the devil.' We believe the Bible ; we are pledged to do so ; we will by no means let down its standards here in the face of the enemy."

And to one of the missionaries he wrote :

"We have got to tell the people the truth, viz. :

"(1) They are bad and going to the bad place to live in torment for ever and ever *because* they are bad.

"(2) If they don't change and become *good*, they cannot go to the good place.

"(3) Are they willing to become good, viz., to forsake all evil?

"(4) If so, there is a way through the love of God, by which way God is willing to hold back the operation of His just wrath against sin and sinners. Two things have to be done :

" (a) Past sins cleansed away.

" (b) Power given to live a holy life.

" (a) By the Blood of Christ.

" (b) By the Spirit of Christ.

"Now the main thing is to get the eyes of these people open. They need to see hell and the result of their sin, and that produces fear, the fear of God which is the *beginning* of wisdom. Once get this fear and all will be comparatively easy ; but if this fear does not lay hold of a man, his socalled conversion is a sham. True love wakens a man to reality ; sham love soaps him down to hell, greases his trail, in fact, to hell. Very many are half asleep or deluded, and make up fancy doctrines of their own, which practically mean that an unholy man can get to heaven without being holy. But remember, Christ did not die to whitewash us, He died to re–create us, and none but His re–creations enter heaven."

With the measuring line of Scriptural standards he measured the thousands of professing Christians now around Ibambi.

"We are all gloriously discontented with the condition of the native Church. It is all very well to sing hymns and go to worship, but what we *must* see are the fruits of the Spirit, and a really changed life and heart, a hatred of sin, and a passion for righteousness. God can do it and we must be content with nothing less ; we need and must have a Holy Ghost storm and atmosphere, and we shall get it. He *is* able to save *to the uttermost* them that go to Him by Jesus. It is also for His glory, as it is also His shame, if Christians, white or black, walk not according to the Spirit of Jesus, and that is the spirit of Holiness and Sacrifice and Service.

"These people want to flee from hell and the devil. They have given up their vile and filthy witchcraft, and that is no small thing. They have got over the Red Sea, they have shouted their hymns of joy, they have reached the desert ; now temptation and the cross have begun to appear, and next murmurings. A leading Christian has been scourged, the cry has gone up, 'All the Christians are being scourged.' Giant Fear has come upon many, so many no longer follow, but have fled. The man himself took it badly, and had a sour face for a long time ; he had no joy in suffering fo r Christ's sake.

"Other ominous signs have begun to make them selves apparent. One of the worst sins of these people is a terrible laziness. To sit about on a chair and talk is the desire of everybody. To work is folly. Wisdom is to leave others to do all the work. The Christianity imbibed by these people has not corrected this ; everyone will shirk if he can. Then, again, their Christianity has not produced love. Where is their love towards God? They will sing of it, perhaps talk of it, but when it comes to sacrificing for God, or working for God, their love becomes a ghost. Then there is a terrible absence of the Fear of God. The Fear of God is to hate evil, and the Love of God is to love righteousness. There are perchance such persons, but verily as rare as the dodo. The general idea seems to be, that they have been baptized, and so washed in the Blood of the Lamb, and are going to heaven, and so it matters not that they lie and deceive and steal and commit adultery and fornication.

"Now where do these people stand? I have no doubt in my own mind, for we are told to judge by fruits, and that 'if any man have not the Spirit of Christ, he is none of His,' and that such as are 'led by the Spirit of God, they are the sons of God,' and 'without holiness no man shall see the Lord,' and 'depart from Me all ye workers of iniquity.'

"Now think of what must be the power necessary to save a man in such surroundings. A man must have a new life, the Divine life, a new heart, a pure heart, he must be a new creation, he must have a Divine love and a Divine hatred. Anything short of this is as ridiculous as trying to cross a hundred yards above the Niagara Falls in a rowing boat.

"Verily we live within an inch of hell and the fumes surround us night and day. And yet, and yet, and yet, *are* we downhearted? HALLELUJAH, NO! GLORY BE TO GOD! We know we shall win by the Blood of the Lamb and the power of His Spirit, and by the help of your prayers. Oh, yes! We shall win right enough, though it may cost a good deal to do so, and the end may easily be that final glorious promise of the Spirit of God, 'They loved not their lives unto the death.' And after all it would be good to die for the Lord Jesus, and for the family, and for these people. But as Paul said, 'Who is worthy of so great an honour?' "

At the same period there arose another serious crisis. There were a few on the Field who were opposed to C.T's strong emphasis on the absolute necessity of practical holiness in the lives of all true believers. There were also a few who were not really willing for the standards of simple faith and supreme sacrifice upon which the Mission was founded, which meant living in native–built houses, plainest of food, no holidays, no recreations, complete absorption in the one task of saving the heathen. There was an undercurrent of opposition to C.T.'s leadership of the work, which finally ended in his being compelled to dismiss two of the workers on the field, and a number resigning.

"While here in the saddle [he wrote], I intend to ride and get others to ride, and not be carried to heaven on a flowery bed of ease. Let us do one thing or the other–either eat and drink, for to–morrow we die, or let us gamble with life and death and all for our Lord Jesus. None but gamblers wanted out here ; let grumblers go home.

"I am getting very fearful lest fizz and froth take the place of the Divine fire among us. I find there is a very real need of solidity among many. I find there is far more talk and time given to food than there should be ; and I find too often that the original foundation of supreme sacrifice gives place to self- pleasing. Ah, we do need to be intense, and our intensity must ever increase. We must always be on the crest of the wave, and all the more because all around are in the trough of the sea of sin.

"Paul loved the music of the Cross. The most wonderful of all God's miracles is this one, that He teaches us not merely to endure sacrifices, but to suffer them with joy and to crave for more. Presently we shall be at the great wedding ceremony of the Lamb, and oh! how we shall want to be clothed in the same clothes as He ; so we must look to it that we have the pierced hands and feet, the thorn–pricked brow, and the wounded and broken heart ; then though we be despised as He was upon earth, and though we despise ourselves, as verily we should, yet we shall not be despised of Him, whom our soul loveth."

These were days of fierce conflict, even some of the Committee at home not being in agreement with him. They put down C.T's uncompromising refusal to parley with those who wanted changes, his refusal to come home himself unless God told him to, his indifference to the opinions of men, his determination to go on along the lines of the first principles of the Mission, though all forsook him, to the effects of fever and strain. The fact was that these were the crisis years of the Mission, the Holy Ghost and the devil in mortal combat, the One to maintain and the other to destroy this instrument for Worldwide Evangelization. C.T., the human founder, was, as it were, the Moses of this Mission. Moses had led a nation of slaves into the wilderness, and there for forty years stood unbending through the fierce testings and attempted revolts, withstanding every suggestion of compromise and backsliding, and in the end by his example and training, left behind him a fighting army, capable of fulfilling God's commission and taking the Promised Land. C.T. did the same for this Mission. Under God he founded it, laid down its objectives and guiding principles, piloted it through its fiery trials, by example and precept trained his co–workers to be good soldiers of Jesus Christ, and has now left behind him an Army of Crusaders, both on the fields and at home, "well able" to go in and possess "the promised land of the unevangelized world," an instrument "sanctified, meet for the Master's use, and prepared unto every good work." Every work of God, as every individual, has to have its period of testing, for only by this means can the dross be purged away, weaknesses and unbelief exposed and eradicated, and the instrument be fitted for effective use. Every work, as every individual, has to go to the Cross, that all that is of man may go to the death, and all that is of God be raised again, unconquerable and to conquer.

The experience was a Gethsemane to C.T. Every now and then his letters echoed both what it cost him to be misunderstood, and how he longed for a new spirit in their midst :

"Sometimes I feel, and especially of late, that my cross is heavy beyond endurance, and I fear I often feel like fainting under it, but I hope to go on and not faint. My heart seems worn out and bruised beyond repair, and in my deep loneliness I often wish to be gone, but God knows best, and I want to do every ounce of work He wants me to do.

"[And in another letter.] What a difference love does make. The Saviour knew it and commanded it. Can't we all love out here? Must we deny our Lord by unworthy suspicion of each other? Suspicions subtract, faith adds, but love multiplies; it blesses twice, him who gets and him who gives. Oh, how I long for love to dominate every soul, when each loves everyone else but himself, and seeks everyone's good, while he goes, like Paul, collecting all other people's sufferings and sorrows to bear them himself. Let this be the rule of H.A.M., then there will be no rules, for the rule of love keeps automatially all good rules. His ministers He has made 'a flame of fire'–not flames, but 'a flame'; for there is and must be a blessed unity, else the Lord cannot bless as He would."

The break came one night in 1925. That night a new Mission was born, or rather the original Mission re–born; and from that night the issue of the conflict has never been in doubt, for God had begun to raise a new generation of "unconquerables" baptized with the same Spirit as possessed those men and women of old, one of whom said, "though He slay me, yet will I trust in him," another, "if I Perish, I perish," and others, "our God is able to deliver us, but if not, we will not serve thy gods."

Bwana come to prayers that night in Ibambi, greatly burdened about the condition of things, and feeling that somehow or other there must come an explosion of spiritual dynamite, which would clean out the hindrances and leave room for the Spirit to work again. There were some eight missionaries gathered with him. They were reading together his favourite chapter on the heroes of faith in Hebrew xi.

"But shall we, can it be possible that such as we shall march up the Golden Street with such as these? It shall be for such as are found worthy! Then there is a chance for us yet! Glory! Hallelujah! Hearts began to burn! The glory of the deeds of these heroes of old seem to scorch hearts and souls. What noble and utter sacrifices they made! How God honoured and blessed them, and made them a blessing to others—then, in their lifetime, yes, and now here to–night! What was the Spirit which caused these mortals so to triumph and to die? The Holy Spirit of God, one of Whose chief characteristics is a pluck, a bravery, a lust for sacrifice for God, and a joy in it which crucifies all human weakness and the natural desires of the flesh. This is our need tonight! Will God give to us as He gave to them? Yes! What are the conditions? They are ever the same, 'Sell out!' God's price is one. There is no discount. He gives ALL to such as give ALL! ALL! ALL! ALL! Death to ALL the world, to ALL the flesh, to the devil, and to perhaps the worst enemy of all—YOURSELF."

But how illustrate so great a matter? The talk turned to the Great War and the heroism of the British Tommy, who went "over the top" at the word of command, and did it, knowing all the odds were against his coming back alive. But how describe this spirit? The question was asked of some who were present and had been soldiers, and one replied, "Well the way the Sergeant major would describe it is that Tommy doesn't care a d—what happens to him so long as he do es his duty by his king, his country, his regiment and himself." Those words were the spark just needed to set the train alight. Bwana arose, raised his arm and said, "That is what we need, and that is what I want! Oh, Lord, henceforth I won't care what happens to me, life or death, aye, or hell, so long as my Lord Jesus Christ is glorified." One after another all who were present rose and made the same vow, "I don't care what happens to me, joy or sorrow, health or pain, life or death, so long as Jesus is glorified."

"The books were closed, heads were bowed once more in silent prayer, then all arose to disperse. But it was a new company that left the hut that night, and by no means the company that had entered it two hours before. There was a laughter on their faces, and a sparkle in their eyes, a joy and a love unspeakable, for each had become a soldier, a devotee to death for the glory of King Jesus his Saviour, Who Himself had died for him; the joy of battle possessed them, that joy that Peter described as 'unspeakable.' "

Many vows of consecration had been taken in the past, but this was something profounder. The Tommy was willing to die though he never saw the victory; the men of faith of Hebrews xi. died "not having received the promises," "not accepting deliverance"; and those who took this vow were now sworn to rejoice in God and shout His praises, not merely when things went well, but in starvation, in insult, in apparent failure, in death, in the fulfillment of their commission to preach the Gospel to the heathen. They had become "unconquerables"; for those who have died in spirit already and by their own choice are beyond being moved by the threats and assaults of the devil, and are already living a resurrected and ascended life, using every test or assault of the devil as more fuel for the flames of faith and praise and love.

It was the Lost Chord of early Christianity revived–those men whose honour was to suffer for Christ, who sang praises with bleeding backs and feet in the stocks, who had the faces of angels and prayed for their enemies when being battered to death by a howling mob.

The blessing spread to the remotest station. From that time to this there has been no check on the field to the unity, love, joy in sacrifice, zeal for the souls of the people, which has laid hold of the Crusaders in the Heart of Africa. Not a murmur is heard, however short funds may be, but only expressions of praise and trust in God. It is hard to get anyone to go on furlough unless health really demands it; and when any do come, as soon as they arrive home, their first question is not "How long can I rest?" but "How can I help in the work here?" and "How soon can I go back?" Married couples put their work before their homes ; one bridal couple, a few days after their marriage, even offered to separate and be on different stations for the time being, owing to shortage of workers. Single women go long evangelizing treks among the villages, where there is a shortage of men; In one district, the worst cannibal in the region, who was reputed to have "a hundred black men inside him," was led to Christ by a single woman missionary who visited his village. Two of the most thriving stations with congregations from five hundred are "manned" by single women only. In some places where there have been only two workers, they have sacrificed human companionship and voluntarily separated in order that one may go further afield and evangelize a new area, although the usual plan of the Mission is to place them in couples. Even in sudden and tragic bereavement they have been triumphant, and glorified God at the grave side, as did one young Crusader who lost his bride but a few months after marriage. He laid her in the grave himself and praised God with such a joyful countenance for her triumphant entry into His presence, and spoke with such victory, that two nuns present admitted afterwards that he had found something in religion of which they knew nothing.

In a short time the blessing spread to the native church. Bwana again led the way by going round and presenting a new challenge to genuine repentance and willingness to leave all sin, as the only basis to true faith in the atoning blood and reception of the Holy Ghost. The challenge bit deep in a way that had never been seen before. The fear of God came on the people. The easy and light way in which many had responded to such appeals before had gone, and in its place was an obvious awakening to the cost of following Christ, and an acceptance of the challenge by one here, and another there, instead of in a mass. Gradually the number increased, but what a difference in them ! Here were the evidences of the Holy Ghost beginning to show themselves, for which the missionaries had prayed and laboured; a brightness in their faces, new life in the praying, a hatred of sin, deceit and impurity, and an exposure of it when found in their midst; the station work began to be done willingly and well; the spirit of evangelism came upon many. "The work is reaching a sure foundation at last," wrote C.T., "and now we willgo bounding forward. Oh, it is good to be in a stiff fight for Jesus." Adzangwe, for intance, one of the worst cannibals and ringleader in all evil, with a face which told its own tale of debauchery, and yet who had been a professed believer some years, was miraculously changed. His whole face lit up. He took the lead in his church of five hundred. He went evangelizing among the surrounding chiefs, and was imprisoned for his testimony, and then got prisoners saved. He and Mr. Studd, though such leagues apart in upbringing, became like two brothers. So inspiring was his example that his church sends out no less than fifty evangelists to-day, all supported by the native Christians, and many to distanttribes. Another Christian was beaten for witnessing, and instead of thinking himself hardly dealt with, rose and wanted to shake hands with the chief for giving him the honour of a beating for Jesus. For that he got another beating, so this time remained on his knees and prayed for the chief. He was thrust into jail; but within a few hours a whole group of his fellowChristians had gone to the chief asking that they too might have the honour of being put in prison for Jesus along with their brother ! Lately, since Bwana's death, fortyseven natives have spent all one night in prayer, saying that they had often dance all night for the devil, and would now pray allnight to God. And so the list might be prolonged.

Thus Bwana began to see the desire of his heart, a holy, Spirit-filled crusader church, in the Heart of Africa. The last five years of his life were now given to getting more and more of the people saved and filled with the Holy Ghost, and spurring them on to fight for Jesus. Only one verse seems to fit these years, "The zeal of Thine house hath eaten me up." He literally lived his vow–lived for Christ and souls. Things that normally take a large place in a man's life were reduced to the absolute minimum or ignored altogether; food just a plateful at odd hours; sleeps, about four hours in twentyfour; holidays, not a day in thirteen years; comforts, the next chapter will describe his "home"; clothes, khaki coat and shirt, breeches and stockings, Sundays and weekdays alike; book, practically only the Bible.

CHAPTER XXI

BWANA'S HOUSE AND DAILY LIFE

THE name "Ibambi" will ever be known in the Heart of Africa as "Bwana Mukubwa's" home. He lived in a circular hut, the walls made of split bamboos tied together with native string, a grass roof and dried mud floor, cracked and patched and repatched. In one corner was a native bed given to C.T. by Chief Manziga. In place of springs it had strips of goat hide tied to the wooden frame. On it were about seven or eight khaki blankets, worn thin with age, which acted some as mattress and some as covering; and at the head a whole pile of hard, thin, canvas pillows. Close to his bed stood a homemade table with an arrange ment of pigeon–holes on it, simply loaded with "gadgets" of every kind, each in its proper place scissors, knives, medicines of all sorts, papers, clocks, spectacles, old Nestle's milk tins full of pens and pencils, etc. On the other side was a shelf full of wellworn Bibles, mostly Revised

Versions. It was his custom to have a new Bible every year so as never to use old notes and comments, but go fresh to the Scripture itself. The Revised was his favourite Version. Such was C.T.'s home, bedroom, dining room, and living–room all in one. How many impromptu meetings have been held at that bedside ! How many midnight and early morning talks, from which missionaries or natives went out to live a new life for God!

Near the foot of the bed was an open log fire on the dried mud floor. At night a black form could be seen curled up on a native bamboo couch as close to the fire as he could get, for it was his only "blanket." This was his "boy." For a number of years the "boy" was a fullgrown man who attended him with the devotion of a woman. He had a stiff leg and so went by the name of "One–leg." Things would begin to move about 2.30 or 3 a.m. "One–leg" would wake up as regular as clockwork, and the first sound would be the beating of the sticks together to knock off the burnt ends, and then the long gentle phoo–oo–oo, as he blew the sparks into a flame in the expert native fashion. Then on with the kettel, and soon a cup of tea would be made. By this time Bwana would be awaked. The tea is handed to him, the boy goes back to sleep again. A Bible is taken down from the shelf, and Bwana is alone with God. What passed between them in those silent hours was known a few hours later to all who had ears to hear. At the native meeting in the morning lasting seldom less than three hours when Bwana took it, at the prayers with the whites at night lasting from 7 to 9 or 10 p.m., what he had seen and heard alone with God in the early morning was poured out from a heart ablaze for the salvation of men, and lips which had been touched with a live coal. He never needed more preparation for his meetings than those early hours.

He didn't prepare. He talked with God, and God talked with him, and made His Word live to him. He saw Jesus. He saw men and women going in their millions to hell. And he always said that is all the preparation a man needs for preaching the Gospel, if it be a dozen times the same day. "Don't go into the study to prepare a sermon," he once said. "That is all nonsense. Go into your study to go to God and get so fiery that your tongue is like a burning coal and you've got to speak."

The daytime would be spent in many tasks. There was the building to be seen to. The ravages of white ants were always eating away the poles and walls, necessitating repairs or new houses. He was particular to the last detail in such tasks as these. Every pole had to be exactly the right length, placed at the right angle, etc.; and he had a purpose in it, for the natives must be taught that good Christianity and lazy or bad workmanship are an utter contradiction. He believed that one of the best ways to teach a native that righteousness is the foundation of God's Throne was by making him see that absolute straightness and accuracy is the only law of success in material things. He put the same concentration and determination to do the best into matters of minor importance such as these, as into his preaching or cricket of early years. If he had a building job on, and it had arrived at the stage in which it needed careful supervision, it was hopeless to wait for him for breakfast. It was 10 a.m., mid–day, and sometimes even 3 and 4 p.m. before he would stop to have food. I have seen him set one of his small boys to search a whole day for one button which the boy had lost, not because he prized the button, but to teach the boy thoroughness and carefulness.

As head of the Mission he had much writing to do, home

correspondence, accounts, a constant flow of letters from the stations, etc. But his supreme joy was to drop these tasks and go out evangelizing. As the work developed around Ibambi, he gave every week–end to these evangelizing trips. They were called "week–ends," but they usually extended on to Wednesday and sometimes Thursday.

Every other Saturday was European mail day. He seldom touched home letters before then, but would start on Saturday morning and have a "field day." All day he would be at his desk writ ing. The other missionaries, who were going out for the week-end, would drop into say good–bye in the afternoon. Still he would be there. Darkness would fall at six. Perhaps at seven or eight he would rise. The mail is hastily packed up, the runner called, given a lantern and a spear, and off through the night for a twelve hour forest walk to catch the outgoing mail runner at Wamba.

Then there was a hast y packing of the few necessities for the week–end, blankets, lamp, book and papers, a few medicines, a few tins of European foods sent to him from home for his own use, but taken out on these journeys and given to the missionaries he was visiting. Some tea and condensed milk, the banjo, a change of clothes, and all would be ready.

Outside ten men are waiting. They are volunteers and picked men, volunteers not because they are not paid, but because carrying at night is difficult and dangerous on the narrow forest tracks, across rivers and badly bridged marshes. Bwana would never allow himself to be carried in the early days; he went everywhere by foot or cycle, and scorned the sedan chair used by all officials and traders. But increasing weakness had made it necessary. His mandala (carrying chair) had a canvas seat in the centre, covered in from sun or rain by native mats, the long carrying poles being made of strong bamboo.

Off he would go, the kapita or foreman leading the way with spear and lighted lantern, the four carriers, two before and two behind, shouldering their burden and singing as they go; and behind them one or two porters bearing his scanty luggage, followed by the spare men for the mandala. Through the night they travel perhaps for four or five hours. By then it may be midnight or 1 p.m. He does not wish to reach his destination, because that would mean arousing the missionaries from their beds, so he finds some empty bandahauri *en route*, a native shed where the people gather to gossip in the daytime, and here they stop and snatch some sleep.

They arrive about 6 a.m. Sunday at one of the big out- stations. Perhaps it is Imbai's, a place that was virgin forest in 1922, and infested with leopards. In early days a patch of forest had been cleared, the "Cricket–pitch church" built, and a little hut for a missionary. Now the whole place has been turned into a beautiful station, with schools, industrial shed, new church, new houses for the missionaries, a street of huts for the natives, and plantations of bananas, pine apples, sweet potatoes, maize and manioc. Imbai, although never as fiery a Christian as some, made a stand before the Belgian officials and Judge which simply amazed them. They summoned him to tell him that he could charge the Mission an annual rental for his land, probably about 600 francs a year, a fabulous sum to an African villagers. But he refused pointblank. He said he had given the land to God. They couldn't believe their ears, and repeated the question, but received the same answer. To–day Imabi's church has about thirty of its own people out evangelizing in the region around and the tribes beyond, all supported by the native Christians.

Bwana often visited them there, The folk would hear he was coming, the news going round for miles, being passed from village to village by the hollow wooden drums upon which they beat out messages to each other. The people would get a bunch of green bananas (their staple food), roll up their little mat, pack inside any precious bit of European cloth of which they might be the proud possessors, and off they would tramp on Sunday morning, men, women and children, when they heard the distant boom of the prayer drum carrying through the forest. Many had hours to come and would not arrive till mid-day. Meanwhile Bwana will have had a cup of tea with the missionaries and an early morning service, perhaps of two hours, with the Christians on the place and nearby villagers. Then back again to the special little bamboo hut which was kept for his visits, where he would lie down and eat some breakfast while the misionaries sat around and talked over all the news with him.

The big service would be about midday. If possible he preferred it in the open under the shade of the palm trees. The people always poured in when he was there, and as many as 2,000 would gather. The meeting begins with a whole hour of hymnsinging, which they loved, the accompanist being Bwana himself on his banjo. Nearly all the hymns (about 200) have been written by himself. If it was a new one or not well known, he would sing a line first, and they would repeat it, until they knew at least the chorus by heart. The better known ones they can sing right through. Many are accompanied by vigorous actions, and when really stirred up, down would go the banjo, and up would rise Bwana from his chair, to lead in a vigorous chorus with shouts of Hallelujah at the end!

Then for a time of prayer, may be for forty minutes, one after another getting up to pray, and raising his hand to heaven as he does so. While one is praying, another stands up ready to start as soon as the first sits down; for if there was not this rule, four or five would be praying at once. At the end of each prayer comes, "ku jina ya Yesu" (in the name of Jesus), which is repeated by the whole congregation. Wonderfully fiery are those prayers too, and probably most end by a public declaration before God and man that they intend to go all the way for Jesus, and praying for the blood to cleanse and the Spirit to fill them.

Then maybe more singing, or a reading and repeating of the Commandments together, and then Bwana speaks. First he reads the Scriptures at some length concerning which he is going to speak, then, standing on the raised earthen platform he talks to them. Usually quietly at first, expounding this and that which he has read, dressing up a parable or Bible story in native fashion, putting the characters into bark cloths and black skins, bread becomes bananas, camels become elephants, snow becomes chalk. Then his whole heart goes out, as he lays bare their own lives to them and the consequences of sin, tells of the love of Jesus, and urges them to repent and believe and follow and fight for Him, if they would get to heaven. He would speak may be an hour and a quarter, an hour and a half, or even two hours. A closing hymn or two, a time of prayer when the call is given for new ones to come and get saved, and then the end when they all rise and with their hand at the salute, say, "God is. Jesus is coming quickly. Hallelujah!"

At night there is possibly a couple of hours over the Word and in prayer with the whites, or another native meeting round a huge fire, made of a great branch of some fallen forest giant. But even that is not all. If you went round, you would find the huts and all available sleeping places full; for many have no intention of letting Bwana off with only two meetings. Have they not brought their sleeping mats and bananas with them? And so Monday becomes just the same as Sunday, and probably Tuesday is given to a great meeting confined to out and out Christians.

The last meeting at which I ever saw Bwana was one of these for out and out Christians at Imbai's in 1931. The Church was packed with a thousand people, about 600 men and 400 women, all of whom had declared themselves as absolutely surrendered to Christ. I shall never forget it, the radiant joy in that sea of faces; the fiery praying led by a withered old black woman in her little bit of bark cloth, but full of the Holy Ghost; the wonderful singing; and finally the hour's talk on the pearl of great price by Bwana, then too weak to stand upright and seated on the arm of his chair.

CHAPTER XXII

HALLUJAH !

THERE was a great sensation among the natives when one Sunday before a congregation of 1,000, C.T. appeared with a new set of shining white teeth. He had had much trouble with his teeth, or the few that remained of them and for some time had only been able to live practically on slops. One day, when some of the missionaries were with him, one of them said, "Bwana, you know you ought to go home and get your teeth seen to." But we knew what his answer would be before he spoke. "If God wants me to have some new teeth, He can just as easily send me some here." We all took it as a joke and laughed, but God had heard! A few months later a dentist in England wrote to the Committee and offered his services for the Heart of Africa. The Committtee considered his application, but finding him ten years over the age limit, refused him. But that did not daunt him. He sold up his practice, with the proceeds bought a passage to the mouth of the Congo, and set off by himself. Arrived there, he began to practice dentistry amongst officials and traders, and in a few months had made enough money to complete the journey into the interior. C.T.'s youngest daughter Pauline and her husband were then on their way home. They were travelling by native canoe, a fortnight's journey on the Aruwimi river down to the point where it joins the Congo. One morning early, as they were being paddled along, they saw another canoe approaching from the opposite direction, making for the interior. In it was a white man. They wondered who it could be, for white travellers were very rare in those regions. As the canoes drew near to each other they called out a greeting in English, to be answered in the same language. It was an Englishman. In a few minutes we discovered that this was Mr. Buck, the dentist, on his way to join Mr. Studd. It was breakfast time, so we drew into the bank, got out into the forest, and had a meal and some prayer together. Then just as we were parting, Mr. Buck took Mrs. Grubb aside and said, "As you are a daughter of Mr. Studd, I would like to tell you a secret that I have told no one else. God has sent me to the Heart of Africa not only to preach the Gospel, but also to bring Mr. Studd a new set of teeth, and I have brought with me all that is necessary for making and fitting them!" Mr. Buck arrived, extracted Mr. Studd's remaining teeth, operating on his mouth so thoroughly that C.T.'s comment afterwards was that he "felt like the poet who wrote :

Gums, gums everywhere
But not a sign of teeth !"

Then C.T. himself tells the remainder of the story : "When

Buck arrived, he said, 'The first thing God sent me to Congo to do was your teeth.' Just fancy God sending a dentist to the very Heart of Africa to look after the teeth of His child, who could not return home!!! What wonder will God not do next?

"I have heard much about bears with sore heads, but just at present I am thinking much more of the poor bears with sore teeth, for the gum are yet unhealed, so the adopted family of my mouth is rather wearing. I can sing much better with the plates in, for so much empty air does not escape and the plate acts as a sounding board, but they get so sore that I have to remove them after a while. Imagine the scene last Sunday. I began the big meeting with teeth all in place. Hallelujahs and wonder. But it was too much, so during prayer I removed them, then as we sang again, you should have seen the faces of the blacks–simply consternation! Who had extracted Bwana's teeth while we prayed? Whenever I appear now, every eye settles on my mouth to see it is their old Bwana or the new one with the teeth. The boys came along the other day, so I put my lower plate lightly in, sat down on a low stool, took up a pair of nippers and pulled out eight teeth with one pull–Tableau!"

The first set never fitted him really well, and as a consequence were often to be found lying on his writing table doing duty as a pen rack. One day he had a narrow shave. He received an unexpected visit from an official. He was only told of his coming when he was a short distance from the house and only just had time to wash the ink stains off his teeth and pop them in his mouth!

Although the new teeth did enable him to eat better, it was obvious that he was gradually getting weaker. Sometimes he had severe attacks of fever, sometimes heart at tacks, and continual suffe ring from bad digestion. Then he took on a task that drained what remained of his strength. He felt that he could no longer leave t he mutlitudes in the regions around Ibambi w it ho u t the writ ten Word of God. In the Welle Province t here had already been a considerable amount of translation done in Bangala, but in the Ituri Province, where the language used was King wana, there was nothing as yet. In spite of the enormous amount of work he was already doing, he determined also to translate the New Testament into Kingwana. It was a marvellous intellectual feat for a man of nearly seventy, quite apart from the weeks of extra work involved. He worked at it night and day. "My day," he wrote, "are eighteen hours as a rule, and no meal but what I gulp down as I write." Much of it was done in the early morning between 2 a.m. and 6 a.m. Sometimes by the end of a day he had such a stiff neck through bending over the table, that Jack Harrison, who was like a son to him, would have to come and gently massage it, before he could sit up straight again. While he translated, Harrison typed. It was a deliberately simple translation, kindly published by the Scripture Gift Mission, made so simple that any bush native who learned to read, could take the book back to his village and understand it.

He finished it, and later also the Psalms and extracts of Proverbs, but at the cost of his remaining strength. Heart attack followed heart attack. Several times he went right to the River's edge. In 1928 he was so ill for a week that it was not though that he could live. At one time, as he lay hardly breathing and eyes closed, it seemed that all was over. But the missionaries managed to summon a Belgian Red Cross doctor, who treated him with various drugs, including morphia. He gradually recovered, but was so weak that he could not get off his bed, nor do any work, still less take meetings, without the aid of morphia. C.T.'s ambition and prayer had always been that he might die a soldier's death on the field of battle, and not be a drag on his fellow–workers through months or years as an invalid. He now realized that the choice lay with him. By continuing the use of morphia he could gain temporary strength to work and preach; the alternative was to be bed–ridden, with one or more missionaries taken from their work to nurse him. He chose the former course without hesitation, and often used to thank God for the gift of a medicine which enabled him to fight for God and the souls of the people to his last breath ; he obtained it from doctors who understood his peculiar circumstances, cut off from all the advantages of treatment in a civilized land, and who considered him a proper person to have it, especially from the Government doctor in the capital. His old friend, Dr. A.T. Wilkinson, of Manchester, who had known him and his physical condition for twenty–five years, and who discussed the matter with him by letter, entirely approved of the continuance of the drug, used, as it was, in medicinal doses for the relief of a permanent disability.

"From early years [writes Dr. Wilkinson] C.T. had been perforce his own doctor, and, in China, dealt medically with others as well as with himself. He was a museum of diseases when he left China, and was afterwards hardly ever free. He understood himself as no other doctor understood him. That he kept himself alive for 70 years, and then did not die directly from any o f his tropical disease, but from surgically unrelieved gallstones and their consequences, is a wonderful testimony to his medical skill. He was ever willing to learn from others, and glad to have medical advice, but he also learned back on the Great Physician; and as regards his hazardous missionary enterprises, did so when on every occasion medical advice was dead against the project. He was a man whom God loved, and took care of–in much the same way as He took care of Paul. Chronic disease calls for chronic treatment. When a man has asthma and recurring malaria and dysentery and the chills and pains of gallstones ever with him in varying combination, what can he do but take the drugs that the Lord himself has provided, to relieve his symptoms, prolong his life, and so enable him to go on with his work? He fought as brave a fight against adverse conditions, within and without, as Paul himself; and in consequence of this judicious treatment he was able to go on working not 8 but 18 hours a day, addressing, often for hours, thousand of his fellow–creatures, telling them of Jesus Christ and the wonders of His Love–and this to the very end of his days. He was one of the finest Christians, and the most heroic and lovable man I ever met."

But only those who were with him can realize the sufferings of t hose last two year s, the dreadful weakness, the nausea, the heart attacks, but, worst of all, those terrible attacks of breathlessness and violent shivering, when he used to turn a dark hue and his heart almost stopped beating ; the cause of this was not discovered till on his deathbed, when a doctor present diagnosed it as gallstones.

Yet the joy of these years far outweighed the suffering, for God had given him to see the two great desires of his heart–unity amongst the missionaries and manifest evidences of the Holy Ghost at work amongst the natives. Aband of some forty missionaries surrounded him, who were like sons and daughters to him. God had fulfilled His promise, "Verily I say unto you, There is no man that hath left house··· or wife, or children, or lands, for My sake, and the gospel's, but he shall receive an hundredfold now in this time, houses··· and children, and lands, with persecutions ; and in the world to come eternal life." At God's command C.T. had left wife and children, and here in his old age God had given him back a family of forty, who loved and attended him with as much devotion as though they were his own flesh and blood. Indeed, it is impossible to describe the bond of affection between "Bwana" and the missionaries, the welcome he received when he visited a station, the constant stream of letters, the loyalty in time of crisis, the family spirit as they all met together during Conference days at Ibambi.

Probably the times with Bwana which will live most in their memory are the nightly meetings at Ibambi. More than anything else they kept the Mission on the true foundation of all spiritual work–the Bible and prayer. There were no time limits, but he just opened the Bible, read maybe two or three chapters, and then talked. The Epistles were his favourites. One hour, two hours, in Conference days till after midnight, night after night, it was always the same, our heart burned within us as we met with Jesus. The greatest of all the lessons that we learned there was that if Christian workers want continual power and blessing, they *must* give time to meet together daily, not for a short, formal meeting, but long enough for God really to speak through His Word, to face out together the challenges of the work, to deal with anything that arises to hinder unity, and then to go to God in prayer and faith. This alone is the secret of victorious and spiritual warfare. No amount of hard work or earnest preaching can take its place.

Motor roads had now been cut through the forest, so that he was able to have a car. This was a great boon, and enabled him to visit all the stations reachable by motor road. These visits were like a triumphal procession, for the natives were so eager to see and hear him, that 2,000 would come where there would ordinarily be 1,000.

In 1929 he heard that his beloved wife had suddenly been taken Home while on a visit to Spain with her friend, Mrs. Heber Radcliffe. The year before she had paid him a flying visit of a fortnight. That was the only glimpse they had of each other. Some 2,000 native Christians gathered to meet her. They had always been told that their Bwana's wife was at home, so busy getting white men and women to come out and tell them about Jesus, that she could not come herself; but when they saw her in the flesh and realized that there really was such a person as "Mama Bwana," they then began to understand, in a way that no words could bring home, the price that Bwana and his wife had paid to bring salvation to them. From that time onward some of the Christians saw in a new way what it cost Christ to redeem them, and what manner of men they must be in the light of that sacrifice. So young did Mrs. Studd look by the side of her husband, that many thought she was his daughter and some mistook her for Mrs. Alfred Buxton ! She spoke a number of times to them by means of an interpreter, and thus fulfilled the prophetic vision she had received after her conversion, when she saw in letters of light on the margin of her Bible the three words, "China, India, Afrcia." The parting was terribly hard, and Mrs. Studd did not want to go, but the hot season was starting and the home end of the work urgently needed her. They said farewell to each other in his bamboo house, knowing that it was the last time that they would meet on earth. They came out together from the house and down the path to the waiting motor car. Not another word was said. She seemed completely oblivious of the group missionaries standing round the car to say good–bye, but got in with set face and eyes looking straight in front of her, and was driven off.

In 1930 C.T. was made a "Chevalier of the Royal Order of the Lion" by the King of the Belgians for his services in the Congo.

A few months before he died he had a glimpse of the summit of missionary ambition, the native church itself catching the missionary vision and sending its pioneers to the tribes beyond.1[5]

There was an insignificant little man, by name Zamu, a member of Adzangwe's Church. He had a large ulcerous wound on his leg, which would not heal and which compelled him to walk on the toes of one foot. He was already a marked man by his fiery praying, consistent life, and keen witness in the villages of his own tribe.

In the spring of 1931 the missionary vision came to this little man. He was stirred by news of tribes in the distant parts to the South. They were his hereditary enemies. Were not these the tribes that killed and enslaved him own people? Would it not be death to go among such people with no protection from the white man? But he had a vision of their souls, he had seen the Outstretched Arms nailed to the cross for the sins of the whole world, and, above all, the Spirit of his Saviour had fallen on him and he had learned to count "the reproach of Christ as greater riches than the treasures in Egypt."

And so one day he came and told Miss Roupell that God was calling him to the "Tribes beyond". She tested him from every possible angle, but to each query he replied by two words. "What about your foot, Zamu? "God is, White Lady." "But the food is quite different, no palm oil, no salt down there." "But God is, White Lady." "You might starve or be killed." "God is, White

5 Much evangelizing had been done by natives in their own tribes, and in isolated instances in distant tribes, but not till now did the native church as a whole begin to catch the missiona ry vision of the trtibes beyond.

Lady." And the biggest test of all, "What about your wife, Zamu?" "She will accompany me. God is, White Lady." There was nothing more to be said, but joyfully to bid him Godspeed. The first stage of his journey took him through Ibambi. It was the last time he saw the old warrior whose life and teaching had so influenced him. Mr. Staniford, who visited him a year later, asked him about that interview :

"What did Bwana say to you?' I asked him. 'Oh, very many things. He turned up the sleeve of his coat and said, "See, Zamu, this arm of mine, once very strong, is now weak, and the flesh shrunken. I can't go with you. My time is nearly finished among you black people. I only go on from day to day as God gives me strength. So don't depend on me, depend on God; He is with you, He won't die, He will keep you." And then he said, "Don't go with shame! Don't be afraid ! Be bold and preach the Gospel! Don't drag the flag of God in the earth! Put it up and don't bring shame upon it! Set your face like a soldier to overcome." Then again, "How many of you are going?" "Just my wife and I." "Well, if you are true, God will make you a great company one day."

Zamu went eighty miles through the forest, across the Ituri river, and then striking due south through the land of the Barbaris, he put another 100 miles between his own tribe and himself. Finally he entered the land of the Balumbi tribe. These people gave him a good reception, but they had never before seen a black man like him who did not gamble, drink quarrel nor live impurely, nor was out to make money, or parade as some important person, so they called him "The Stray Man." Their friendliness soon cooled, however, when they discovered that the message which he preached cut right across their sins. He and his wife would have starved, had it not been for the brother of the chief, who had received the Word gladly, and took Zamu to his garden and told him to help himself freely to the plantains, cassava root and spinach growing there. But courage, faith and love won the day. In one place opposition was broken down by Zamu kneeling on the ground and tending the feet of a sick old woman whose toes were being eaten by dozens of "jiggers," and who had been left to fend for herself, even by her own relations. The insipid food, without salt or palm, fat, became their greatest trial, and finally he asked the Lord to send them a little luxury, "O Lord, you have kept your messengers from starvation, but we long for a little salt. Send us this as a token that You are with us." The answer was indeed beyond their dreams. Unknown to them other members of his home church had been stirred into action by his example, and just at the very time that he prayed that prayer, the first party of reinforcements were leaving to join him. One day, a fortnight later, he saw a party of strangers coming down the village street, and then recognized them. What greetings and what joy! News from home, old friends united, reinforcements, and, to crown all, a large packet of salt–a gift from Mrs. Grainger.

Where Zamu went alone in 1931, there are now some ten evangelists scattered among the Balumbis. But his venture of faith has had more far–reaching results than even this, for it has kindled the missionary flame throughout the native church ; numbers have volunteered, and already some fifty native pioneers and their wives have penetrated to all points of the compass, entering some six new tribes.

In a letter home, C.T. gave a last backward look at the outstanding events of his life;

“As I believe I am now nearing my departure from this world, I have but a few things to rejoice in ; they are these :

“1. That God called me to China and I went in spite of utmost opposition from all my loved ones.

“2. That I joyfully acted as Christ told that rich young man to act.

“3. That I deliberately at the call of God, when alone on the Bibby liner in 1910, gave up my life for this work, which was to be henceforth not for the Sudan only, but for the whole unevangelized World.

“My only joys therefore are that when God has given me a work to do, I have not refused it.”

Of all the native Christians there was none he loved more than the converted cannibal, Adzangwe, and his love was returned in full measure. One of C.T.’s last visits was to Adzangwe’s church. Adzangwe was a dying man. He was far gone in consumption, and the pallor could be seen beneath his black skin. He lay on his native bed in his little bamboo hut on the outskirts of the busy station, which five years before had been virgin fo rest, when he had given the land to be “a place fo r God.” Once when Miss. Roupell visit ed him to sympathize wit h him in his suffering, she was met with this greetings, “You must not look sad when you come in here, white lady, because I am not sad. As I lie on my bed, I talk with God and He talks with me, and Jesus Christ is round about me like the walls of my hut. I talk with Bwana also,” (for he had his photo pinned up on the wall in front of his bed); and his radiant face bore out the But sick and weak though he was, as soon as he heard that his beloved Bwana had come, nothing could keep him in his hut. He called for some help from neighbouring huts, was lifted into a chair and carried over to the missionaries' house, where Bwana was sitting. Bwana came out to meet him while one of the missionaries brought a chair for Bwana to sit in, and some cushions to make it more comfortable, for he was himself as weak and emaciated as Adzangwe. But before he would sit down, he took the cushions from his chair and packed them round the body of the converted cannibal. It was a picture in miniature of the One who though He was rich, yet for our sakes became poor, and Who came not to be ministered unto, but to minister. That was the last time they met. For some months Bwana had been having a special joke with him. He told him that they were having a race to Heaven, and that he intended to get there first. If Adzangwe did win, then he would "have a row" with him when they met up there. Only about three weeks after, Bwana won the race.

The end came suddenly. Mr. Harrison gives us the details :

"Ibambi, July, 1931.

"By the time this reaches you my cablegram will have arrived, telling you that Dear Old Bwana has gone to be with his Lord. First of all let me assure you that through it all there has been the ring of Victory, in Bwana himself, in the missionaries too, and more than all in the natives. Oh, how we do praise God for this.

"On Sunday last (12th) Bwana seemed very fit indeed. He told us all to get off to the different places of worship in the district, as we usually do on the Lord's day. He himself alone remained for the native service here on the station. On our return in the mid-afternoon Bwana was still ever so fit and to our amazement told us he had a *five–hour* meeting!!

"On Monday (13th) afternoon, he asked me to give him an

injection of quinine as he felt cold and thought may be he had some fever hanging around, although there was no temperature at all. In the evening he felt still worse and I stayed with him all night until 4.30 a.m. During that night he had very much pain in the stomach towards the right side. He told me that evening that he suspected gallstones, and asked me to read up all I could about this complaint. I did, and to our amazement, we found that in every detail the symptoms agreed with his case. On Tuesday morning he was still weaker and in very much pain too; and in the evening still weaker and the pain ever so severe··· On Thursday morning (16th) he was easier and thought that the pain in the stomach had moved somewhat. He had become so weak and exhausted by this time that now his voice began to weaken. He tried again and again to speak. We got very little of what he was saying. We could only tell by the expression on his face as to whether we had guessed his wishes aright. In the early afternoon we caught something about 'Heart bad.' Mr. Williams asked him if he thought he was going to leave us this time, and at first he said he didn't know, but shortly afterwards he said, 'very likely.'

"From that moment onwards there was no question about it –he ceased to try to talk about anything and with each little breath he could spare he could only say "Hallelujah!" "Hallelujah!" It was amazing to see him passing out like this–quite conscious all through and just Hallelujah' coming with every breath he had. How wonderful too that we could not make out his other words properly because of the weak voice, but the 'Hallelujah' none could mistake, and even the natives around the bed could hear this!

"At about 7 p.m. on Thursday he seemed to lapse into unconsciousness, and shortly after 10.30 p.m. passed to his reward. It was a fine going. He was smiling all through except when the actual pain seemed to grip him again. Even in his extreme weakness he was concerned about Elder, who had had an ingrowing toe nail cut just a few days before, and was telling him to go and rest his foot. The last time he was with the natives at service was the five–hour one last Sunday, except for his usual morning prayers with his boys and a few others round his bedside on Monday morning. The last native he really pressed to get right with God was Chief Kotinaye. His last written word in a letter to the missionaries was 'Hallelujah.' The last word he spoke was 'Hallelujah' too!

"The boys were very good indeed. Isatu and Boyo and 'Jim Crow' were ever so faithful, and also Ezeno and Boimi. We worked all night Thursday preparing a coffin and they did ever so well. Hundreds and hundreds of natives came in at once to ask to see him. So in order that they might have a last glimpse of him, we had a 'Lying in state' in the front room of Bwana's house. Hundreds filed past the coffin and ever so reverently too. We covered the coffin with the Savita' (Soldiersaint) flag that Bwana himself designed long ago–it looked splendid and was very fitting too, for Bwana was 'Savita' indeed. He had been rightly named 'Bwana Mukubwa'–the 'Big' Bwana–for he was in every way big. Big in what he thought and did, big in suffering for others, big in faith, love, sacrifice and devotion to his Saviour. Big in the knowledge of his God and the scriptures. A veritable giant spiritually, before whom we appear as dwarfed as the pygmies of our Congo forest.

"The natives who were closest to him carried him to the graveside and the white men missionaries lowered him down. God gave wonderful liberty. There stood about 1,500 to 2,000 blacks, including Chiefs Kotinaye, Owesi, Abaya, Simba; what an opportunity for the Gospel!

"As the grave was being filled in, recording angels were busy in heaven registering the vows that were being made and renewed there. And then in the large prayerroom of Bwana's house, where they had had so many exhortations from his own lips in the past, the missionaries linked hands all round and sang :

"Standing by the Cross,
Standing by the Cross,
We shall help each other,
Standing by the Cross.

"The natives who came in on Friday for the burial would not go away again. We had a splendid meeting on Saturday with them, and oh, the prayers! We had never heard the like from blacks before. All seemed to have the same thought in their minds, that of reconsecrating themselves to God and saying that in spite of Bwana having been taken, they were going on hotter than ever for Jesus. To–day also (Sunday) We have had larger crowds than ever. It is the Lord's doing and marvellous in our eyes."

CHAPTER XXIII

GOD ENABLING US, WE GO ON

IS it outstanding personalities that build up a work of God, or is it the Holy Spirit working through surrendered lives? There were a great many people who really attributed the success of the Mission both at home and on the field to the unique personalities of its founders, Mr. and Mrs. C.T. Studd. They used to wonder what would become of the Mission when they had gone. C.T. and his wife, on the other hand were never in any doubt about it. They knew and declared their own nothingness, and that all that had been done was the work of the Spirit of God, which He will do through anyone who will utterly believe and obey Him. C.T. was thinking of that when he nicknamed himself and Alfred Buxton, on their first journey to the Heart of Africa, "Balaam's Ass and Noah's Dove." Was it personality or was it God the Spirit that founded this Mission and carried on this Crusade? Now was the time to see, for both the "personalities" had gone to their reward. Our founders had been taken; not a single person remained on the staff of the Mission whose name bore any weight with the Christian public ; the home end of the work had just passed through a crisis ; and as a last straw it was the time of the great financial depression throughout the country. If the force behind the Crusade was really the founders' personalities, then all hope was gone.

My wife and I were the sole representatives of the Crusade at Home, and we decided that we would put the God of our father and mother to the test. In times of greatest trial they had staked their all on the faithfulness and sufficiency of God, and we would do the same. "Where is the Lord God of Elijah?" cried Elisha, as he took the cloak of his master and smote the water with it, "and they parted hither and thither ; and Elisha went over." We believed that the only memorial they would wish for would not be one in stone or glass, but in flesh and blood, which would glorify God and further the evangelization of the heathen. So we decided to ask God to do what was to us in our existing circumstances an absolutely impossible thing, a thing which if guided by common sense instead of faith, we should not only maintain the existing work, but also give us twentyfive new workers and the money to send them out (about £3,000), ten by the first anniversary of C.T.'s death, and fifteen by the second ; and in order to prove that it was God alone Who did it and that He is the same faithful God to all who trust Him, we covenanted with Him that we would make not a single appeal to men, nor any effort to get either men or money, but depend solely upon prayer and faith. This is what happened :

"We began praying for 'The Ten' in November, 1931, and were that same month able to send out the first two. There was only sufficient money for their passages, but they volunteered to go straight out so as to start on the language, and in faith that money would come for the remainder of their equipment within a few months.

"It was not until January that the full conditions of believing prayer were revealed to us from God's Word, and we were given grace to obey them. We saw that the men of faith in the Bible, by whom God did impossible things, always fulfilled one condition beforehand–they demonstrated that they had really believed God by openly stating beforehand what He was going to do, in full assurance that He would do it. The Bible abounds in instances of this, such as Paul on board ship in the storm, when God had assured him that they would all be saved, and he publicly told them to cheer up, saying, 'I believe God, that it shall be even as it was told me.' We did this first of all by publishing among our own inner circle that God was going to send ten missionaries by next July (the first anniversary of C.T.'s death); then by writing to the field and telling them to prepare for ten new workers during the summer ; and finally by publishing the fact in the magazine.

"March came, and by now we had three lady candidates ready to go out, but no money–we faced the situation together, realizing that now the time had come to receive a deliverance from the Lord, and believed that He would give it. Two of the ladies went away for the Easter week–end, but in faith they left their addresses with the third, so that she could wire them if the Lord sent the money. On Saturday there were two guests at the Mission House. So far as we knew, they were people with no spare money in the bank. But as a matter of fact unknown to everybody they had a small sum laid aside which they had dedicated to the Lord years before, but

He had never told them what to do with it. Before going to bed, a few minutes were spent in prayer, and in one sentence someone mentioned the need of the three. No more was said, but God had spoken; the guidance which they had waited for for years had come, and next morning they told us that the money was for the three. It turned out to be enough for two passages. At dinner time we made the news known and said that we must send the wires. But here came the faith of the third, who had not gone away, into action, for she said, 'Why not wait half an hour? God may yet send the money for the third passage!' This was said in spite of the fact that it was Sunday, when no post or visitors were expected. That same hour someone had cause so go into the Mission officer, which is usually not entered on Sunday, and there found a letter. The address was Lady's Club in London, and inside was a cheque for £100 ! Numbers 3, 4 and 5 of the Ten sailed on May 26, taking wit h them the completed equipment of Numbers 1 and 2.

"By this time two more young men had offered, fully trained ; and about the same time a sufficient supply of money had come. They sailed very shortly after the ladies in June, number 6 and 7 of the Ten. In the same month a lady arrived from Canada, bringing with her about half the sum needed for her outgoing, No. 8.

"And now for the last lap. Six weeks remained, and no application, and no money for the remainder of the Ten. Five weeks, None. Four weeks, No application, but a gift of £100. Three weeks, still none. Two weeks, No. 9 applied, a fully trained lady with nursing experience. Now there were but days left. Thirteen days, twelve, eleven, ten, and on the evening of the tenth a fully trained young man applied as No. 10. It was at a conference at the Bible College of Wales, Swansea. He had spent three days in fasting and prayer to be sure of God's call, and the very next day the Lord set a wonderful seal on his application, and a wonderful completion to The Ten. There was a guest at this Conference who knew nothing about the offer of this young man. When praying before breakfast next morning, the Lord led him to take a blank cheque from his chequebook, and put it in his pocket, but did not reveal to him what it was for. At breakfast he heard the news about No. 10, and at once the Lord told him that the cheque was for this purpose. Shortly after he gave the Secretary a cheque for £120.

"Two days later two of us were in Ireland. We talked together and came to the conclusion that it would be a complete answer if the Lord would send £200 more, so we agreed to ask Him for this in secret. Two days after, as we came out of the meeting, our hostess handed one of us a telegram, and although she had not the faintest idea about our secret prayer, said, as if in a joke, 'Perhaps there is £200 in it.' when the telegram was opened, it read, '£200 for the Ten, Hallelujah!'

"And now there remained fifteen to be sent by the second anniversary, July 16, 1933. We wrote a leaflet telling the story of The Ten, and at the end of it declared our faith that God would send The fifteen by saying. 'God has sent ten in one year, and we believe that He will send the other fifteen in the next year.'

"For the next five months God tested us greatly. We had expected a flow of candidates, but half the year went by and not one was ready! So impossible did it seem that the whole fifteen should come in half a year that we decided to ask God in December for a special seal on it. It was lack of faith on our part to do so, we ought simply to have believed ; but in spite of this, God wonderfully answered. We asked Him to send us £360 during

December for various special needs. December 30 arrived and only £200 had come. The magazine had to go to the press on December 31. Was I to publish an article saying that The fifteen would come by July, or not? while in prayer I suddenly said to the Lord, 'If You will only send £100 before 11 a.m. tomorrow, I will take that as a seal. But if you don't, I will not put in the article.' Eleven o' clock next morning came. I had the magazine proof on the desk in front of me–but no £100. So I said to the Lord that I was very sorry, but under the circumstances I must drop The Fifteen and not publish about them. As I said that, I saw the Business Secretary coming across the garden. He entered the room, waving something in his hand. It was a cheque from Scotland for £100! And the article went in !

"The next few months things began to move quickly. The first three men sailed for the Heart of Africa. Then came the most important revelation of all. The Ten had been only for the Heart of Africa, and we had looked on it that The Fifteen would be the same. But through the remark of a friend, our eyes were suddenly opened to the fact that as God's commission to Mr. Studd had been a worldwide one, the most perfect thing would be that the 'Memorial Twentyfive' should be world–wide also. We then woke up to the fact that although there had been only three men for the Heart of Africa, in the last few months we had received applications for no less than four other unevangelized fields–Colombia (South America), Arabia, Little Tibet, and Spanish Guinea (West Africa). And then we realized the full sweep of God's plan and provision, that the first ten should go to the land of Mr. Studd's special labours, the Heart of Africa, and the last fifteen to be scattered through many lands, and continue to carry out his world–wide vision of occuping every unoccupied region with the Gospel. Two came forward for Colombia, two for Arabia, two for Spanish Guinea, three for Little Tibet, and one more for the Heart of Africa. This made the total up to thirteen.

"The Lord had sent money for some of these. Especially remarkable was the gift He sent for Mr. Pat Symes, the first pioneer to Colombia. Although he was going to a field totally new to the W.E.C., the Lord had clearly told him not to rely on deputation work to obtain the needed money, but trust Him alone. A few days after, he made a public declaration to that effect. That came day he only had *6d.* in the world and was sent an errand to the other end of London. He said nothing and went. He spent *4d.* in getting part of the way there. On the ways back he walked part of the way and intended getting a *2d.* bus ride, when a 'down–an–dout' on the Embankment begged the price of a cup of coffee. Pat refused, saying that he had only *2d.* in the world, and passed on. But the Lord told him to go back and speak to the man about his soul. He went back, but found he could not speak to him about his soul and do nothing for his body, so the *2d.* changed hands, and Pat walked seven miles home. He arrived weary and perspiring to be met at the door with the news that God had sent £100 for him during his absence, and during the very time that the devil was busy telling him what a poor business the life of faith was!

"Now only six weeks remained. There were still two more vacancies in The Fifteen, and about £500 needed to send them out. The Prayer Letter for June had to go out. We told how The Fifteen stood as far as numbers were concerned, but without mention or hint of the money needed, except to say, 'God will complete it. The shorter the time left, the more wonderful will be the deliverance.

Join us in praise and faith and expectancy, and look forward to the next Letter telling the story of the final deliverance.' On June 15 we went down to the Bible College of Wales for our Annual Conference. On arrival at the station we were met with the news that two more fully trained young men had received the call for Colombia. Thus the number was complete. All that remained was the £500. The next day the Lord took me to the verse, 'If ye abide in Me, and My words abide in you, ye shall ask what ye will and it shall be done unto you.' He showed me that the person who was consciously abiding is given the right by God to claim that promise. I took it for the £500 to come during the Conference.

"The Lord always tests faith, and the test came the following day. I was asked if I would attend some days of prayer in Ireland shortly after the Conference. I knew I could not go away before The Fifteen was completed and the money in, therefore the only possibility of acceptance would be if the £500 came in at the Conference. What was I to say? I said I hoped I would come. The Lord said, 'That is not fait h. Hoping is not believing.' I tried again and said, 'I will, if the Lord has sent the deliverance.' The Lord said, 'There are no "ifs" about faith.' The Scripture says, Faith is substance (Heb. xi. 1), and the man of faith acts on faith just as if he had the current coin in his pocket.' So the Lord helped me through and I said, 'Yes, I will attend the prayer days, because the deliverance is coming at the Conference.' "The last day of the Conference.'

"The last day of the Conference came, and not a penny. Next morning we were all dispersing to return home. The morning post brought £50 for Colombia and I received another gift of £10 for the Fifteen. We were thankful for £60, but it was a long way from £500! Farewells were said, and people began to leave for the London train. It was found that there were many more for this train than were calculated, and there were not enough conveyances.

Just at the last there was still a party waiting to go. A large taxi was got hold of. We went in with the party and were driven off at top speed. Half way along the three miles' journey a tyre went with a bang! We all jumped into a tram, but it was too late. We arrived at the station to find the train just gone. Ten minutes were taken making fresh arrangements, and then one of those who had lost the train took me aside and said, 'How much is in for the Fifteen?' 'About £60,' I answered. 'Well, that is my seal, for the Lord told me yesterday that if there was still need today I was to give £400.'We left the station, and not five minutes after were in conversation with a friend and telling him the glorious news. He took my arm, 'I will give another £100,' be said. A few hundred yards down the street again and another friend said. 'I am going to give you £30.' 590 in half an hour from five different sources, not one single one of whom was a wealthy person. We were like them that dream. Then were our mouths filled with laughter and our tongues with singing."

But even this, the completion of the "Memorial Twentyfive"1[6] within the two specified years, is but part of the blessing that God has poured out on the group of "Insignificants" who are carrying on the works, and but part of the proof that the secret of C.T.'s life was not a great personality, but an Almighty Person completely controlling him.

---

6 1 In 1934 a second 25 was sent out ; in 193537 50; in 193s 40 75-a total of 17 to fourteen fields.

We have already told how Mr. and Mrs. Studd had deliberately entrusted both their own lives and those of their children to God, and how He had kept His hand on the four girls, how all had been converted, how He had provided for their education, and how three had married men whose lives were wholly given to the service of Christ. The husband of the eldest had been a brilliant soldier, commanding a regiment and winning a number of decorations in the War, but had never surrendered to Christ. He and his wife came home from Rhodesia two years before C.T. died, and were living temporarily at the Mission House in Norwood. Gradully he became more interested and accepted an invitation to Keswick in 1931. At the evening meeting on the Thursday, July 16, at the very hour when in a bamboo house in the heart of Africa C.T. was breathing out his last hallelujahs as he entered into the presence of his Lord, the appeal for surrender to Christ was made in the tent at Keswick, and C.T.'s son–in–law, Colonel David Munro, was among those who rose to their feet. The last gap in the family circle was filled, and all eight, the four daughters and sons–in–law, were united with their father and mother in their allegiance to Christ.

Finally, we turn to Africa and have a last glimpse of the missionaries and natives just a year after Bwana had been taken from them. Mr. Harrison describes the scene to us, and with his description the book will close. Did C.T. make the best use of his life when he left all and followed Jesus? Is God faithful to those who do so? Is it a fact that if a man gives the Holy Spirit complete control of his life, rivers of blessing flow out from him to the world (John vii. 38, 39)? Is it a fact that a life lived in the centre of God's will is the only life that can satisfy man's deepest aspirations and put his powers to their fullest use? And the only life that will enable him to say at the end, "I have fought a good fight?" This book is an answer.

On the first anniversary of C.T.'s death a Native Conference was held at Ibambi. If we had felt the loss of our Founders at home, how much more on the field, where "Bwana" had stood head and shoulders above his co workers in the eyes of the natives. As many as 4,000 had come to a Conference with Bwana, but how many would come, now he was not there? Now would be seen the extent to which he had drawn the people about himself or pointed them to Christ. Mr. Harrison writes as follows :

"Some said, 'The work has been built on Bwana's own remarkable personality.' Others put down his success as a missionary to the fact of his 'family', or his 'natural gifts.' Others added, 'He has gone–the work will go too; he has died–it will die with him.' But what saith the Lord? 'Their works do follow them.'

"And what have we seen? Collapse? No! Retrenchment? Never! Only advance, deepening, establishing and fruitbearing from the life laid down. The native and white Conference we have just had is abundant proof of this. Thousands and thousands came–far more than we have ever seen before. Some are positive there were 8,000 people present, but estimating the number as only 7,000 to avoid all possibility of exaggeration, this would mean that there were twice as many as at any previous gathering. With such a mixture of tribes and clans, it can easily be understood that things might get out of hand. But, glory be to God, from the very beginning it was just a miracle how the Lord kept them all so quiet and so happy. Mabari and Mabudu jostling together with Mazande and Medje, Mangbettu and Mayogo with Marambo and Malika! Can you just picture it? Truly the Gospel is breaking down their tribal prejudices. It was just a glimpse of the greater Day round the Throne, when every tribe and nation shall bow the knee before the Lamb.

"The blessing of the Lord was with us whites also. Each morning and evening as we gathered round the Word, we knew that Jesus Himself drew near. And never a discordant note. Oh, how we praised our Saviour for the fires that have so welded us together. On the evening of July 16, the first anniversary of the homecall of our beloved leader, we met together for a time of heartsearching around the Lord's table. As we remmebered the Lord's death, and in thought went back to the night of Bwana's passing on, we were constrained to renew our vows to God and to one another. Never would we lower the standard shown in the Word! Never would we break the fellowship in the Gospel! Never would we cease our labours for the furtherance of the Gospel! Should we have less blessing in the future? Need we have less? Shall we have less? No!! For the Blood shall never lose its Power, and the Spirit will always lead to victory, and we shall, God enabling us, Go on!"

C. T. Studd

Man of Faith

This printing 2018
Published 2012 by WEC Publications

PO Box 137 Seo-cho Post Office
WEC
www.goimm.org

ISBN 978-89-88432-08-2 03230

Printed by CORAM DEO Seoul Korea
02.2264.3650 ~1 PRINTED IN KOREA